Advance Praise for
Reflections from the Field

Insightful, informative and practical, DeMeulenaere, Cann, Malone and McDermott provide a blueprint for understanding how to engage important lessons from coaching in the classroom. Using first hand experiences, these authors brilliantly weave their personal accounts of coaching into a fabric of theoretical insights, and useful strategies for practitioners. Each of these chapters will push teachers to think beyond conventional pedagogical strategies, and free them to explore the power of the "coach" within them.

—**Shawn A. Ginwright**
Author of Black Youth Rising
Associate Professor of Africana Studies
San Francisco State University

The best teachers—intuitively or consciously—find ways in their daily practice to inspire, illuminate, encourage, demand, model, illustrate, provoke, co-create, exemplify, and clarify, all the while recognizing that the stars of the show are the students and not themselves. They know that teaching is harder than learning in one fundamental regard: teachers must know how to let students learn.

Through story, personal essay, oral history and memoir *Reflections from the Field* is an invitation to meet a set of teachers who recognize what it means to *let learn.* These folks are reflective practitioners, relationship-builders, and also, not coincidentally, coaches—they know how to improvise, how to nourish and challenge in a single gesture, how to recognize the uniqueness of each and the power of all, and how to dance the dialectic between thought and action.

This vivid kaleidoscope offers teachers an opportunity to see how it's done, and to consciously reconnect with what's fundamental about the whole educational enterprise.

—**William Ayers**
Author of To Teach
Distinguished Professor of Education and Senior University Scholar (retired)
University of Illinois, Chicago

I am thankful that DeMeulenaere, Cann, Malone, and McDermott provide us with a candid view of what it means to be successful coaches and teachers. Their work is further testament to the fact that we cannot in good conscience send teachers into the current morass of political madness without support that is critical, constructive and affirming. In the political moment that threatens what it means to be a facilitator of thought, skills, and actions, may we all be enlightened by their failures and triumphs in standing for equity, solidarity and justice.

—**David Stovall**
Co-Author of Teaching Toward Democracy
Associate Professor of Education and African-Studies
University of Illinois, Chicago

Reflections from the Field

How Coaching Made Us Better Teachers

To Jock —
My adopted Big Brother —
a teacher in his own right —

Jim

Reflections from the Field

How Coaching Made Us Better Teachers

Eric J. DeMeulenaere
Clark University

Colette N. Cann
Vassar College

with

Chad R. Malone
and
James E. McDermott

INFORMATION AGE PUBLISHING, INC.
Charlotte, NC • www.infoagepub.com

Library of Congress Cataloging-in-Publication Data

A CIP record for this book is available from the Library of Congress
http://www.loc.gov

ISBN: 978-1-62396-268-5 (Paperback)
      978-1-62396-269-2 (Hardcover)
      978-1-62396-270-8 (ebook)

Printed in the United States of America

To Salihah and Jai, who are doing their math "homework" while mama/aunta writes this dedication when we're supposed to be at the beach already.

And, to the little one on the way,
we can't wait to have you join mama/aunta camp!

—Colette N. Cann

To my mom, my first coach.

And to Susan and Mykah and Tyla for being my guides on the side.

—Eric J. DeMeulenaere

Contents

Foreword

In the second decade of the 21st century, we are in the throes of a great debate about the nature of teaching and teachers—what teachers need to know, what makes for a good one, how they should be prepared, and how they should be treated once they are members of the profession. On one hand, there are proponents of the emphasis on accountability, teacher evaluation and testing, and the need for getting rid of bad teachers. This is the dominant view of the U.S. government (under Republican and Democratic leadership—No Child Left Behind and Race to the Top, respectively), and a leading view among policymakers, foundations, politicians, and pundits (Kane, 2012; Gates Foundation, for example).

A very different view, however, is gaining prominence—captured well in the vision of what Finland did (over the past 40 years) in radically rebuilding its educational system. That view is captured well in Pasi Sahlberg's (2011) book, *Finnish Lessons* (see also Partanen, 2011; Ravitch, 2012). This view emphasizes "responsibility" and professional competence over "accountability." It emphasizes belief in the professionalism of teachers, not their micromanagement. Rather than testing students and teachers, or using mechanisms such as choice and charters, value-added assessment techniques for evaluating the worth of a teacher, or merit pay, the approach is to recruit the best and the brightest into teaching, and train them in a rigorous and rich university-based course of study, and then to provide ongoing support in the field, so that lessons from the field emerge and contribute to the lifelong learning and improvement of teachers, teaching, and learn-

Reflections From the Field, pages ix–xii

ing.[1] It's quite simply a diametrically opposite path toward recruiting and supporting teachers, building the field of education into a respected and respectable profession.

The U.S. seems to be heading—fast and furiously—down the path of accountability, union-bashing, and the deskilling of teachers (emphasizing short-cut Teach for America approaches for recruiting and training novice teachers, and the privatization of education through charters and choice, as dramatized in "Waiting for Superman"). A few prominent scholars (such as Linda Darling-Hammond, Diane Ravitch, Deborah Meier, and Mike Rose) are trying hard to wave the red flag and get our attention. But whatever Finnish lessons there may be, we seem, as a society, not to be learning them.

In the midst of the heat of these debates, I received a prepublication copy of *Reflections from the Field: How Coaching Made Us Better Teachers*. It seemed at first—excuse the pun—to be coming at me out of "left field." A book about team sports and athletic coaches? Knowing nothing about school sports and having no interest in them, I was puzzled. And then I started reading, and simply couldn't put the book down. I read the book in one sitting, transfixed by the narratives of visionary coaches/educators (the odd chapters), which were then supplemented and extended by the commentaries and research evidence (the even chapters).

The title, *Reflections from the Field*, is an apt play on the word "field." It is a book about and by coaches—really coach-educators—and it uses the power of story (tales from the playing fields) as well as non-narrative research (reports from the field of educational research) to provide a very different lens on teaching and teachers. These narratives are inspirational and offer practical insights into the construction of pedagogies that don't confuse classroom management with teaching.

We are taken from a baseball field into an English classroom where student athletes are described by their principal as "losers" both on and off the field. We observe in this narrative, a skillful coach-teacher employing a pedagogy of trust to build a winning team despite the low expectations of the administration. This same pedagogy, so successful in building a winning team, proves critical to engaging the same student-athletes in the classroom.

In the gym, we overhear an athletic director complimenting a girl's basketball team on the losing end of a 90–6 outcome. The coach-teacher, angered by the false and insincere comment, is motivated to take over coaching the team, offering honesty and the focused coaching necessary to turn the team around. This same coach-teacher later realizes that he, too, had been guilty of offering false and insincere compliments on his students' papers in his classroom. He takes the lessons learned on the court into his classroom, bringing honesty, time, and targeted instruction to improve the writing of his students.

In another gym on the opposite coast, we witness a volleyball coach build a winning team from a group of initially mediocre players by strategizing creative and necessary on-court relationships among players. These relationships decreased status differences among players and built a culture of mutual respect. These lessons, when brought into a heterogeneous mathematics classroom, built a community that accommodated status differences among students and became a space where learning could happen.

Finally, out of the soccer field, a coach learns to develop leadership on the field that can inspire and mentor novice players to construct identities as fierce and fearless athletes. These lessons, later applied in the classroom, create opportunities for students to support each other in their academic growth and learning.

In reading these narratives and their adjoining commentaries, I was reminded of Jerome Bruner's (1986) dichotomy between two forms of thought and meaning making, described as two modes of cognitive functioning. The first is what Bruner calls the narrative mode—which leads to compelling stories and accounts, by which believable worlds are created and understanding, not necessarily truth with a capital T, emerges. The second is called the paradigmatic or logico-scientific mode—a formal, rational, and systematic mode of description and explanation.

Reflections from the Field harnesses the power of both modes of thought moving back and forth between compelling narrative accounts of coaching students in a variety of contexts and sports, and critical commentary on these narratives, citing educational research and providing conceptual and explanatory constructs that help make sense of the stories; of the forms of powerful interactions, missteps, accomplishments; and ultimately of the transformation and learning that took place (learning on the part of students and the coaches themselves). The narratives are riveting and moving. At some points, I had tears in my eyes and had to read through the blur. The non-narrative text is another view on coaching and its relevance to teaching, reflective *on* and *in* practice, providing a complementary way of understanding and generalizing from the narrative accounts.

I found myself sharing these "reflections" with my most valued colleagues in the field of education—mathematics educators, learning scientists interested in the Next Generation Science Standards, and researchers interested in classroom discourse, professional development, pre-service teacher preparation, policy and evaluation! *Reflections from the Field* is quite simply a tour de force—in both style and substance—one of the most powerful books on teachers, teaching, and learning I have read.

Compelling, useful, emotionally inspiring, and cogently argued with evidence, the book will change you as you think about teachers, their knowledge, and their value. It should be read by every pre-service teacher in the U.S., every teacher-educator, and every practicing educator. Then we will have a different base, a new view of the game, from which to build. The book provides a foundation (with both narrative and evidential cogency) from which to decide whether the responsibility or accountability lens is most likely to succeed. And in it, we have a touchstone text to help us develop the inner courage and the political will to make the changes necessary to build a profession built firmly on *reflections from the field* (in both senses of the word).

—**Sarah Michaels**

Note

1. In Finland only 1 out of 10 applicants is accepted into a 5 year BA/MA training program, with the last 2 years required for the MA. Finnish teachers are supported with opportunities for professional learning with mentors and colleagues, time to plan and think and learn, and autonomy derived from professional respect. And they receive good pay, good working conditions, and the material resources to teach well.

References

Bruner, J. (1986). *Actual minds, possible worlds.* Cambridge, MA: Harvard University Press.

Chilcott, L. (Producer), & Guggenheim, D. (Director). (2010). *Waiting for "Superman"* [Motion Picture]. Hollywood, CA: Paramount.

Kane, T. (2012, June 24). Should student test scores be used to evaluate teachers? *Wall Street Journal.* Retrieved from http://online.wsj.com/article/SB10001424052702304723304577366023832205042.html

Partanen, A. (2011, December 29). What Americans keep ignoring about Finland's school success. *The Atlantic.* Retrieved from http://www.theatlantic.com/national/archive/2011/12/what-americans-keep-ignoring-about-finlands-school-success/250564/

Ravitch, D. (2012, March 8). Schools we can envy [Review of the book *Finnish Lessons*]. *New York Review of Books,* Retrieved from http://www.nybooks.com/articles/archives/2012/mar/08/schools-we-can-envy/?pagination=false

Sahlberg, P. (2011). *Finnish lessons: What can the world learn from educational change in Finland?* New York, NY: Teachers College Press.

Preface

Iam blessed to have many gifted teachers in my life. I come from a long line of educators and am surely not the last. My great grandmother, legend has it, crossed flooding rivers to teach classes in her one-room schoolhouse. I remember very little about my great grandmother, Our Own Hardy, except that she was short, fierce, and a powerhouse whom you hesitated to cross in argument or on the street. My paternal grandparents were both New York City teachers, with my grandfather moving into administration as a school leader. From as early as I can remember, he would bring over certificates because I had eaten my vegetables and, thus, joined the "clean plate club," taking pride in even the smallest of achievements. I got my love for and facility with numbers from my grandmother, ever ready with a book of math puzzles and a sharpened yellow pencil; to this day, I have no idea how they stayed sharp at the bottom of her large brown purse. She'd lick the point on the pencil, open the book breaking its spine, and hand them to me, saying, "Here, Nikki. Let me see you do this one." If I got stuck, there was the patient explanation, the example, working it out with me and then sending me off on my own. Even after she retired, I remember students coming up to her flat, going into the small room off the dining area to work on their homework after school. My maternal grandfather, a master carpenter, apprenticed me into my love for power tools and all things wood. When he passed away, I heard from others at his services how he took on young carpenters and taught them the trade.

Reflections From the Field, pages xiii–xviii
Copyright © 2013 by Information Age Publishing
All rights of reproduction in any form reserved.

Perhaps my greatest teachers have been my sister, mother, and father. Five years younger, my sister ran behind me with her own fat red pencil asking for me to give her "homework." I taught her to play the sports I loved better than I ever played them. Her total trust as I said impatiently, "Just jump backwards! I'll catch you. You think I'm going to let you fall on your head?" taught me more about teaching than any school of education. I sought to find the right metaphor for her to hang new information on to her existing schema or break a volleyball skill down into smaller chunks only to put them back together into one fluid movement—trial and error as a teacher with an ever-patient student.

My mother is the teacher I know I need to be sometimes. Her own brand of fierceness elicits a terror surpassed only by the fear of what might come if you don't do what you need to do. When I've procrastinated to the point of being ridiculous, she was the enforcer, holding me accountable to the work I said I'd complete. In our older years, she looked over our shoulders less, but her hands-off reminder, "Well, it's up to you. You know what's going to happen better than I do if you don't get that work done tonight," was all that was needed to remind us that our goals would not be achieved if we didn't buckle down in that very instant. She was also the one who, with a fair bit of sighing, grumbling, and (in my opinion) unnecessary commentary, stayed up with us to finish that project that she'd warned us to start on weeks earlier. Never an athlete, she nevertheless came to practices and games—sometimes cheering at the wrong times, but always our biggest fan. She held us accountable and provided the support when we fell short. It was almost never pleasant, but always appreciated.

My father is the teacher I strive to be. He can find an example that can clarify a complex concept in a matter of seconds. He can sketch detailed illustrations with a finger in the sand of a long jump pit that adds inches to your very next attempt. He is my own personal magician who snatches the exact metaphor I need from an invisible space behind my right ear. On the track, the volleyball court, or at the kitchen table, a sleight of his hand would illuminate the very concept that would unlock a secret I had already known.

He hoped that my sister and I would pick a sport that he knew something... anything... about. We grew up inhaling the basic skills of basketball and exhaling the mechanics of how to explode out of sprinter starter blocks. Those were his sports and, ever in hopes of accompanying him on his weekend warrior trips to the courts or track, we willingly tagged along. We watched him shoot the basketball three feet from the basket hundreds of times, making subtle changes until it felt right. "Ok, so did you see what I did there? I moved my elbow in—that did it!" Mostly his monologue fell on ears that had long ago tuned out to these brief comments, but we heard the hard work and dedication necessary to master a skill.

Fear of being left home trumped our fear of scaling 15 foot fences to get onto basketball courts to watch our dad play pick-up games on the weekends. A chorus of baritone Black male voices encouraged us as we slowly made our way up one side leaving my father's arms and down the other side into the arms of players who, only minutes later, would be arguing over some foul or another. My sister and I would watch as my father and his buddies ran the court, talked smack, boxed out, bumped celebratory elbows and fists, and told each other what to do and where to be. When he was done, he'd coach us on our own shots or play two-on-one, easily throwing out compliments, never critique. Just wasn't his style.

When we were old enough to choose our own sport, we chose volleyball. Though he had never played nor watched volleyball prior to his "California girls" picking it up, he didn't miss a beat. He jumped right in as our first "personal trainer." After volleyball games, he'd ask questions about what we did, how we did it and why. "So, I saw you do that thing with your hands. What was happening there?" He studied the game as intently as he followed basketball.

He made parallels with basketball to help us with positioning. Unable to play volleyball, he would jump-shoot the volleyball, basketball-style, into the air so that we could practice our hitting. Again and again, he tossed balls to the left, right, over our shoulders, and almost out of reach in front of us. We would explain what a skill should look like and he would act as our mirror: "Wow! That looked really good, Nik. Just like you said it should look."

"But, dad, what did I *not* do right?"

"Uh, well, it looked good to me. I don't think it can get better than that." And I believed him because he believed that I, in that moment and every moment, was perfect.

—**Colette Cann**

My mom is strong. She is athletic, tough, and competitive. When I was a child, our neighbor from across the street arm-wrestled her. He was incredulous that my mother claimed she could beat him at arm-wrestling. He was humbled when, after giving his all, she touched the back of his hand to the table. After years in the weight room and joining the Marines, he came back to prove his manhood against her. Even then, she didn't just roll over.

When I was three, my mother and her twin sister, who lived across the street, would organize the neighborhood kids into big wheel races and all other kinds of athletic events on our cul-de-sac. My athletic mom grew up in a time period when class and gender discrimination meant the only sports offered for girls in her school were classes that taught the skills of basketball, softball, dancing, and so on, but there was no type of inter-scholastic competition. So when I was little, she was my first coach working to organize the competitive tournaments she felt excluded from as a child.

Mitchell Elementary School, typical of many suburban schools at the time, was filled with middle-class White children whose fathers mostly worked and whose mothers often stayed at home. So a lot of mothers volunteered at our school. Most of the moms helped in the ditto room, decorated bulletin boards, or tutored at the back of the classroom. I am sure my mom did some of that too, but what I remember most was that my mom organized the after-school sports activities with my aunt. When first grade let out, my classmates and I would run out to the baseball diamond where she would bring out those red rubber all-purpose balls for kickball tournaments.

Unlike the kickball games we kids would try to organize at recess that would take forever to get into teams and usually dissolve into an argument before the second inning, my mother organized us quickly and kept a tight order while we played. She would guide us to our positions, keep score, and silence disputes. I learned from her the importance of structure. She would not allow any disrespect. Players who challenged her would be sitting alone behind the backstop. It only took a couple of examples for us all to learn the rules. With her in charge, we were safe. Even if you fell down, the other kids knew better than to point and laugh at you.

But while her strong presence maintained a welcome order, the order increased rather than dampened our fun. We had a blast. The game would last a long time and we never wanted it to end.

Matching my mom's tenacity for protecting us all from teasing was her patience as a teacher. I remember waiting for my turn to kick as I looked through the diamond-shaped openings of the chain-link backstop. An uncoordinated kid was up to "bat." He had no idea what he was doing. He stood on home plate holding his straightened leg back like a wooden stick. The pitcher pitched it and he swung, his leg missing the ball entirely, his timing completely off. You could hear the sighs from others in line. But a quick stare from my mom made it clear our mouths would stay closed.

My mom picked up the ball and rolled it back to the pitcher with the instructions to "roll it very slowly."

He still missed.

She rolled it back to the pitcher and instructed the boy to back up from the plate and run up to kick it.

He took a small step back and she went and guided the boy back ten paces with her hands on his shoulder.

"Okay, nice and slowly," she commanded the pitcher.

The ball inched along the ground. I rolled my eyes while my mom's eyes were focused on the awkward boy. He just stood there.

Tapping him gently on his back she instructed, "Run and kick it."

The ball bounced against his leg and nearly tripped him.

My mom grabbed up the ball and, holding it under her arm, she repositioned the kicker. She placed the ball on the home plate spot. She held the boy's hand and ran forward with him to kick the ball. He kicked it with his toe and it bobbled out into the field. The pitcher ran forward to get it. My mom hollered, "Run, run, run!"

He started running towards first base, and the girl who was playing pitcher ran and easily tagged him.

The boy turned around with big excited eyes, not at all upset that he just caused my team an out. My mom exclaimed, "Good job, I knew you could kick it." The boy smiled back as he scooted back in line.

In the little kick-ball league that she started, my mom showed a lot about what it means to be an effective coach and an effective teacher. Order and structure were important. Both learning and fun required a safe and structured environment. She also revealed the importance of patience. Failure just becomes a guide for how to try something different; it is not any reason to get upset. Patience lets you keep working to figure it out. Also, encouragement is critical. People can accomplish a lot when others believe in them. Encouragement helps us begin to believe in ourselves.

My mom's greatest gift to me was encouragement. I tease my mom today for looking through the world with rose-colored glasses. My mom is so wired to see the good and potential in other people that she is easily duped. Even though she grew up in a fairly tough neighborhood in San Fernando and is approaching seventy years of age, she is still noticeably shocked when she encounters intentional deceptions or hate crimes in the world. But while I can tease her for her distorted view, I know that I, as her child and lifelong student, am deeply blessed by it. Seeing an image of myself projected through her eyes did something to me. I grew up seeing myself through her as a smart, moral, and capable human being. I didn't want to disappoint this image she conjured up for me, so I strove to become her projection.

She has believed so strongly in me and has been so blinded to my flaws that I have become a much better person because of this vision, this encouragement. That image has willed me to my greatest achievements. When others believe in us, we slowly learn to believe in ourselves. And it is remarkable what people can achieve when they are encouraged to believe in themselves and when they are given confidence and courage by others.

This is a book about coaches who encourage their players. It is the story of four athletic coaches who learn to become better teachers taking their lessons from the field and applying them in the classroom. All four find ways to get their players—to get their students—to believe in themselves.

—Eric DeMeulenaere

1

Introduction

The use of the coaching metaphor in the field of education has become widespread (Heath & Langman, 1994). A recent search of the Education Resources Information Center (ERIC) database for articles with the word "coach" in the title produced over one thousand citations. Despite its widespread use, the coaching metaphor rarely draws direct lessons from the athletic arena to an academic one. The metaphor instead serves as a euphemism to either connote the shift from traditional, didactic instruction to a more student-centered and constructivist pedagogy or from top-down school reform to democratic, site-based reform (Murphy & Datnow, 2003; Neufeld & Roper, 2003).

The coaching metaphor first came into use in educational theory over 25 years ago when Ted Sizer pushed classroom teachers to coach their students, modeling the relationship between athletic coaches and their players. He argued, "The only way to learn to think well and usefully is by practice. The way a teacher assists this learning is by coaching" (Sizer, 1984, p. 216). In this book, we pick up this dropped thread to consider the direct connections between athletic coaching and classroom teaching, with a focus on the significant implications of sports coaching for improved pedagogy.

Reflections From the Field, pages 1–10
Copyright © 2013 by Information Age Publishing
All rights of reproduction in any form reserved.

To do so, this volume presents several narrative accounts written by former coaches of baseball, basketball, soccer, and volleyball. These coaches were also classroom teachers of English, mathematics, and social studies. These narratives reflect what these coach-teachers learned from their coaching experiences that transformed their classroom pedagogy. They recount their struggles to create winning sports teams and elucidate the processes of working through these challenges. Each narrative chapter then importantly connects lessons learned on the field and court to specific pedagogical practices implemented in the classroom to transform the learning of students, particularly students others had given up on. Following each narrative written by coach-teachers, we analyze their stories in light of educational research and policy.

Sporting Insights

Although Sizer's use of the coaching metaphor in education quickly departed from any direct connection to athletic coaching, there is a growing body of recent literature that has examined more explicitly the connection between coaching and education. Drewe (2000) argued that the dichotomy between "education and training" leads to the false assumption of a similar dichotomy between teaching and coaching. In fact, the dichotomy between education and training might not be appropriate either, and she sought to dismantle both dichotomies in her article.

According to Drewe, education refers more broadly to interaction with and development of a "belief system," while training refers to the teaching of a particular skill necessary to achieve an identified outcome (p. 80). This dichotomy is assumed to carry over into the distinction between teaching and coaching. Communication skills are identified as important to teaching, whereas knowledge of one's sport and motivational techniques are considered important to coaching. The assumption is that teaching is about teaching along multiple dimensions—fostering the student's social, emotional, and academic development. In coaching, though, the assumption is that the only dimension of importance is that related to developing skills to win. These assumptions often lead sports coaches to focus on the concrete skill development and team development that pushes the immediate goals of building a winning program. Yet Drewe proposed that much might be gained if coaches took education and teaching as central to their work. She explored the similarities (and differences) between physical education teachers and sports coaches to understand how we might think about what coaches have to learn from teachers. She suggested that coaches might learn to teach the whole athlete, focusing not just on skill development, but assisting youth in thinking critically about values, morals, ethics, collaboration, fairness, and treatment of others.

Holt (1999), an English teacher who, midway through his teaching career, began coaching football, also made a connection between his coaching and classroom teaching. Though he began his coaching career without any coaching experience, he had hoped his teaching experience would translate onto the field. He found, though, that what he did on the field actually produced a greater impact on his classroom teaching—"teaching and coaching are two sides of the same educational coin" (Holt, 1999, p. 16). He found that as a coach, he often physically demonstrated positions, methods, and skills for his players; he got off "the sidelines." Similarly, he found that in English class, too, he must demonstrate writing. Showing students the writing of established authors only is akin to showing his football team a pass by John Elway—it doesn't show them the struggle behind the writing. So, he decided to share his own writing and writing process with students, arguing, "[I]t makes all the difference when your students see you doing the same activity you have asked them to perform. And frankly, they need to see the activity performed to the degree of proficiency that they can realistically hope to achieve" (Holt, 1999, p. 5). In addition, he learned the importance of practice and focusing on critical points rather than overwhelming new writers with too many rules of writing.

Glenn (2002), in her interviews of coaches (both sports and business) and players/employees, similarly found that there are skills and successful techniques that coaches use to motivate and direct their players and employees that might benefit classroom teachers. These included, for example, the statement of team and individual goals, presence, and enthusiasm, and the creation of a space where players can take risks. Coaches who articulated a team vision and goals, who had a larger-than-life persona that motivated athletes to push themselves, and who refused to tolerate language and behavior that embarrassed or humiliated others (making it difficult for them to take risks going forward) created winning teams with players who exceeded expectations. Glenn contended that what players learned about themselves and their potential for excellence from their coaches was beneficial to students as well. Interviewed athletes noted that what they gained from their coaches would have benefited them in the classroom as well— that their teachers should implement similar strategies.

Gallimore and Tharp (2004) wrote a seminal article titled "What a Coach Can Teach a Teacher" on the pedagogical practices of famed UCLA men's basketball coach, John Wooden, who led the team to ten NCAA championships. In this article, they reanalyzed data from their 1976 study of Coach Wooden, included a new interview with Coach Wooden, and took into account newer studies of Coach Wooden's practice that had been published since their initial analysis, including an autobiography by Coach Wooden. As researchers in education and psychology, they were interested in studying the pedagogical practices of a master coach. In Coach John Wooden, they found a reflective practitioner who invited their study of his practice in his final season.

In observing practices and interviewing Coach Wooden, they first found that he did not rely heavily on compliments and reproofs to motivate and teach his students. Rather, he leaned on "explanation, demonstration, imitation, repetition, repetition, repetition, and repetition" (as cited in Gallimore & Tharp, 2004, p. 132). During the explanation and demonstration, he used the "sandwich model," showing players how he wanted a skill done, showing the incorrect way to do it, and then re-showing how it was done (Gallimore & Tharp, 2004, p. 124). He also tried to give the overall picture of what they were going for, broke it down into its necessary parts, taught those parts and then rebuilt it to the whole (Gallimore & Tharp, 2004).

Further, Coach Wooden believed in repetition to ensure automaticity—not to "drill and kill" the creativity and individuality of players; rather, the more solid players were in their skills, the more options they would have in games: "[F]or him the purpose of drilling automatic skills and habits is to create the foundation on which individual initiative and imagination can flourish" (Gallimore & Tharp, 2004, p. 133). Coach Wooden explained in a personal interview with the researchers:

> I never wanted to take away their individuality, but I wanted that effort to put forth to the welfare of the group as a whole. I don't want to take away their thinking. I wanted options. I wanted a second and third option on most of the plays that we would set up and I wanted our plays to come within the framework of our general overall philosophy and not say you have to do this, you have to do this, and you have to do this. This is the general idea, but the other team may have some ideas too and we've got to have a choice, you have to think for yourself sometimes. (as quoted in Gallimore & Tharp, 2004, p. 133)

Perhaps most important, Coach Wooden modeled on-court and off-court behavior and took his responsibility as a role model seriously. A quote that he found in the 1930s stayed with him throughout his career: "No written word, no spoken plea can teach our youth what they should be. Nor all the books on all the shelves, it's what the teachers are themselves" (Gallimore & Tharp, 2004, pp. 133–134). His former players and students concurred that he had a profound effect on their lives because he taught about life, not just basketball or English. Duncan-Andrade (2010) adds,

"Wooden insisted that his players prioritize their excellence as human be-ings, a trait that is not typically emphasized, or measured, for teachers or coaches" (p. 44).

One important distinction that doesn't have direct implications for the classroom, perhaps, is Wooden's strategy of only playing the 7–9 strongest players on his team unless an injury forced him to play one of the reserves. His rationale was that these players needed to know each other and each other's playing styles well enough to work seamlessly as a team. The reserves played an important role—albeit not on the court—to keep the central play-ers in shape and help them practice plays. In one sense, this tactic meant that everyone played a critical role on the team—starters and reserves alike. On the other hand, the inherent inequity (assuming that each player's goal was to play in games) created status differences on the team.

To counter these status differences, Coach Wooden publicly reward-ed reserves during practice more than the central players (who, Coach Wooden argued, received compliments from the public while playing). He reasoned that the reserves needed his compliments to keep coming out for practice and giving 100%. However, in Gallimore and Tharp's (2004) research, some of the reserve players and Coach Wooden himself acknowl-edged that he didn't give those compliments as often as he had planned, and status differences were not diminished. Coach Wooden said in a per-sonal interview:

> A player one time said, "You never let me play with Alcindor (Abdul-Jab-bar). I can do better if you let me play with him. Now you have me with some rinky-dinks." I told him one time, "That's what somebody said about you when you were in there. You were one of the rinky-dinks." By practicing and playing only 7 . . . I don't think it made for better harmony for the team as a whole. It made for better harmony . . . among the seven regulars that are going to get the actual playing time. (Gallimore & Tharp, 2004, p, 131)

In a later communication with the authors, Coach Wooden admitted:

> Looking back, I think I sometimes failed to get reserves to feel how impor-tant they were. Over time, some of my players began to tell me that. My in-tentions were to make the reserves feel important to the team, and I thought I did. I guess I was fooling myself. (Gallimore & Tharp, 2004, p. 131)

In a similarly titled book, *What a Coach Can Teach A Teacher: Lessons Urban Schools Can Learn From a Successful Sports Program*, Duncan-Andrade (2010), an English teacher and basketball coach, had the opportunity to interview Coach Wooden. From that interview, Duncan-Andrade pulled two points: to "[treat] everybody differently under the same set of rules" and to "[keep] things simple" (p. 45). Of the first, Duncan-Andrade explained, "What Wooden emphasized to me was that our standards had to be dynamic enough to respond differently to the unique talents and needs of each student, without sacrificing those standards—everybody treated differently under the same set of rules" (Duncan-Andrade, 2010, p. 45). Of the second, he wrote:

> Teams that are good at many different aspects of a game will certainly win their share of contests, but eventually they will lose to teams that have formed a culture of greatness around a few essential aspects of the game. This simple advice changed how I coached, and how I taught my English classes, by forcing me to narrow my teaching down to a very few areas that I believed were indispensible to greatness. (Duncan-Andrade, 2010, p. 46)

Though the coaching metaphor seems to be upheld in these few available studies, Stellwagon (1997) argued that the teacher-as-coach, though accurate in some ways, is over- and misused to the disadvantage of the teaching profession. First, coaches often work with a select population—those who are the most talented, skilled, and voluntarily present. Players more often than not try out for their teams, and only those most committed and talented are recruited for the team. Thus, unlike many classroom teachers, Stellwagon contended that coaches don't have to work with whoever shows up.

However, we argue that some teachers, like some coaches, do actually choose the student population with whom they work. Through teacher tracking (Cann, 2012) and student tracking (see for example, Oakes, 1985), teachers are able to determine the students they teach. Equity-minded teachers (such as Joan Cone, see Chapter 7 in this volume) and coaches (such as the coaches in this volume) work with any student interested.

Second, Stellwagon found that coaching is appropriate to the teaching of skills, not the instilling of values and development of intellect. Thus, to imply that coaching is applicable to all instances of teaching and learning is misleading.

Countering Stellwagon's point, though, some coaches, such as Coach Wooden and coaches on Glenn's panel of expert coaches, argued that instilling values is central to the work of coaches and is a vital part of their coaching pedagogy. Coach Wooden, for example, viewed coaching as programmatic rather than simply techniques of guiding and modeling. For him, it was very much about knowing one's student/player population and developing the whole player.

Finally, Stellwagon contended that comparing teaching to coaching contributes to the further deprofessionalization of teaching; coaches often bring very little training as coaches to their positions. They are likely to have played the sport as an athlete, and that is considered enough to be offered a coaching position. Arguing that teachers should be more like coaches, according to Stellwagon, is akin to arguing that anyone who was a good student of a subject can teach that subject without further training in pedagogy, educational theory, methods, and classroom discipline. Certainly programs like Teach for America rely on this, recruiting from top colleges that graduate students who "can do" school with the assumption that this will translate into effective teaching.

However, here again, we can find coaches who are extremely prepared for their post, who take the preparation seriously—attending workshops, interning under more experienced coaches, and continuing to reflect and grow as coaches. We can also find those coaches who do no preparation and learn on the job (and, thus, on their athletes) and who leave the coaching profession shortly thereafter. Similarly, we find that diversity in the teaching field as well.

The Authors

This book engages the reader in narratives of coach-teachers who achieved acclaim for their teaching and credit many of their insights to their experiences as coaches. The first narrative is written by James E. McDermott. Coach McDermott grew up in a working-class Irish neighborhood in Worcester, Massachusetts. He was able to secure a college degree on scholarship and emerged from college with a degree in English. Not knowing what to do, he took a job as an English teacher in the Worcester Public Schools. Committed to his students whose lives reminded him of his own growing up in Worcester, he worked to figure out how to reach his students. He credits his coaching baseball and football and running the drama program with teaching him a lot about how to best reach students. He was a quick study and became an exceptionally popular and effective teacher. He eventually won the title of State Teacher of the Year. After teaching and coaching in Worcester for over thirty years, he recently retired from teaching. His narrative explores the beginning of his baseball coaching career, taking over a team that had not won a single game the previous season. His players did not lack talent as much as they lacked guidance. The players had internalized the school's label of them as a group of players and students going nowhere. Coach McDermott's story shows the requisite creativity and faith in his players' potential that moved his players to believe in themselves.

Chad R. Malone, the author of our second narrative, became a teacher and coach in 2005. He was raised in a small New Hampshire town, the son of a contractor and teacher. As a high school student, he proved academically strong in the classroom and proficient on the basketball court. His increasing awareness of social inequality led him into teaching where he quickly brought his basketball skills to bear, volunteering to coach while a student teacher in Worcester, Massachusetts. That experience landed him a job in a nearby school, one of the lowest performing in the state. He quickly became one of the most beloved teachers in the school and, in his second year, was voted by the faculty as Teacher of the Year. In Coach Malone's narrative, we see how he took over his school's basketball team after they suffered a humiliating defeat. Through his honest and bold leadership, he led the same team to compete in the district playoffs two years later. Through his experience he learned the importance of coupling love with an almost brutal honesty.

Colette N. Cann, the author of the third narrative, has diverse teaching experiences as a coach and teacher. She grew up a volleyball athlete in Los Angeles. As a young Black woman at an elite and predominantly White private high school, she felt a disconnect that ultimately caused her to leave the high school. She eventually landed at a Catholic school that embraced its racial and cultural diversity. There, she continued to play both varsity and club volleyball through graduation. In college, she played intramural and tournament volleyball. After graduating, she taught mathematics in both elite private schools and urban public schools. She also coached junior varsity volleyball, was assistant coach for a varsity team, and coached club volleyball. She went back to school to earn a master's and doctorate in education, winning a teaching award as a graduate student for her work teaching undergraduate education courses. She is currently an assistant professor in education and Africana studies. Through her mistakes and successes, Coach Cann's narrative explores how she learned to organize a team through building interdependence and a recognition of the different roles and abilities of each player.

Eric J. DeMeulenaere, the author of the final narrative, grew up in the White middle-class suburbs of Southern California, but spent his high school years in Anchorage, Alaska where he attended public schools and played varsity basketball and soccer. After college, he taught history and English for a decade in middle schools and high schools in Oakland and San Francisco, CA. While teaching in San Francisco, he helped to start a girls' soccer team. Building this soccer team taught Coach DeMeulenaere that coaching doesn't happen only from the sidelines. Indeed, effective coaches and teachers, he learned, develop the leadership of youth on the field and in the classroom.

Format and Methods of the Book

We employed narrative inquiry to examine the complex social contexts, cultural norms, expectations, and practices in the classroom and on the field (Burdell & Swadner, 1999; Chase, 2005; Denzin, Lincoln, & Rolling, 2006; Ellis, 2004; Wall, 2006). These rich narrative accounts capture the complexities and subtleties of effective practices in complicated environments. We used narrative inquiry as teacher-researchers to study our own practices and push the development of our practice (Duncan, 2004; Duncan-Andrade, 2010). Narrative inquiry, as a reflective and reflexive process of telling, analyzing and representing, provides a space to narrate stories and study them rigorously for what they have to offer others.

In Chapters 1, 3, 5, and 7, the authors narrate their coaching and teaching stories, providing examples of successful coaching practices. Each of these chapters is followed by a commentary chapter that analyzes the story to cull larger themes from the narrative and connect these themes with educational theory. The two concluding chapters frame these narrative accounts and the concrete lessons from coaching and sports more broadly to discuss to what degree the coaching metaphor serves as more than just a metaphor.

How to Read This Book

We wrote this book as much for ourselves as coaches and teachers as for others. As has been argued (Bolton, 2010; Ellis & Bochner, 2000; Harris, 1989; Melany, 2007), writing is thinking. It provides an opportunity for reflection, for codification of process, and, as most of the authors continue as educators, for praxis. This book brings together our own thinking about how coaching has influenced our classroom teaching.

We wrote this book also for current practitioners. We believe that there are lessons to be gleaned from our narratives, the analyses of these narratives, and the connections made with educational literature that can assist in the further development of individual teachers' and coaches' practice. Just as we attempt to grow in our own practice by pulling from the experiences of others, we hope to offer fodder for reflection in others.

We hope that, in reading this book, readers will be drawn to and inspired by the narratives first just as school leaders, teachers, and coaches are drawn to the stories and experiences of others (Brill, 2008). These stories provide support and affirmation often, as well as warnings and lessons learned. Debriefing one's day in the teacher's lounge among teacher friends is familiar to educators. Our own narratives may appeal to this need to hear the stories of other educators.

We also, though, encourage readers to sit with the accompanying commentaries. Each narrative is followed by a commentary that makes the more explicit connection between coaching and classroom teaching, bringing in educational research to underscore important practices. While narratives are powerful, we also realize that it is through reflection and analysis of such stories that transformative meaning-making occurs. We hope readers will bring their reflections from the narratives to engage with the commentaries as a sort of dialogue to further thinking. We include the educational theory not to rationalize practices, but to open the discussion about why particular practices work in different settings.

As well, we believe strongly that theory is a part of the praxis process in which great coaches and teachers engage. Coach Wooden, master pedagogue, coach, and English teacher, perhaps best exemplified the role that deep reflection played in his continuing efforts to hone his craft and his attempts to improve his practice from season to season. He took his craft seriously and put the necessary work into being prepared to develop individual player skills and the dynamics on the team. All of his practices were planned to the minute, the drills and his comments were purposeful, his instruction was player-specific, and he kept copious notes to assist in further planning.

Duncan-Andrade, a researcher-teacher who engages in reflective practice, discussed the importance of theory to his own teaching and coaching. He wrote,

> For the first five years of my career, I rarely intellectualized my work in this way. However, my mid-career return to graduate school taught me one of the most valuable pedagogical lessons I have learned—the value of theorizing and intellectualizing our work as educators. (Duncan-Andrade, 2010, p. 9)

We hope that readers, too, find in the following narratives echoes and inspirations for their own teaching and/or coaching practices. We also hope that they find here ideas and tools for theorizing and intellectualizing their own practice.

$$2$$

Winning Has Little to Do With the Score

James E. McDermott
Clark University, Worcester, MA

In my English classroom, I had the "at risk" kids. On the ball field I had the "losers"—labeled students and players who believed the labels. Teddy and Ares were the students who symbolized for me that changing the culture and expectations in the classroom and on the field can inspire students and players to aspire beyond ascribed labels—can transform kids caught up in the trivial, the mundane, and the common into those who see the possibilities of their own brilliance.

Teddy was playing third base; I was pitching: "Come on Coach. Fire it in there. Got the corner, Coach." It was tryouts; I was the new coach, my first time outside, dots of diminishing snow banks, dirty along the heavily shaded areas, flurries in the air. As I wound to throw another pitch, my eye caught Teddy, a cigarette burning from his mouth, dangling on that same lip that continued to voice hustle and encouragement for his new coach.

Reflections From the Field, pages 11–19
Copyright © 2013 by Information Age Publishing
All rights of reproduction in any form reserved.

Stopping in mid stride, I bellowed, "Teddy, you've got a butt in your mouth! Take a lap around the field."

Dropping his glove, he immediately began running. Winding up to fire another pitch, I halted when the batter dropped his bat, laughing and saying for all, "Look at Teddy!" Teddy was still running, jogging hard, butt in his mouth, lighted, little puffs following him. I knew right then that all the time I had spent working on plays and batting and fielding and running and sliding and such would not be my first priority.

* * *

In the beginning, Teddy and Ares and his mates would "yes" me to death while continuing to pull stunts. For example, during one game early in the season, we were playing a terrific team, a private school with a huge fan base, getting beaten very badly, when I noticed in the middle of an inning that I did not have a right fielder. "Where's Teddy?" I asked the players on the bench. They pointed to the foul pole where Teddy was relieving himself—Teddy was peeing while the pitcher threw, batters swung, and fielders covered, all except for the right fielder, of course. I whispered to the guys on the bench not to point or otherwise call attention to Teddy. I was embarrassed. Teddy wasn't. "When nature calls, Coach," he said with a shrug.

Teddy would never have made it with my high school coach. In fact, Teddy would have been thrown out of my Catholic private high school because as silly as Teddy behaved on the field, he was even sillier in the classroom, always doing something to call attention to himself, never studying or completing homework assignments. His classroom competition was Ares—for class clown. Both could fake read and fake do assignments, but neither understood that their attitude and spunk and imagination and creativity and thinking could be used to transform them into excellent students. Schooling and thinking to them were mutually exclusive.

The principal called Ares the "worst piece of shit" he had ever seen and was angry I selected him for the team. That same principal had placed him in my low-tracked English classroom, so why should I exclude him from my baseball team? He was 16. I am a teacher. That's what we do. Teach youngsters. "You'll be sorry," insisted the principal.

Ares and Teddy and their mates were tough kids from tough neighborhoods, one of whom would be shot twice before he was twenty. That group of youngsters swore more than a congregation of Marine drill sergeants. I had to figure out how to address the language problem. Threatening them would never work. So one practice I gathered the team together, announcing that from now on, only one person on our team would be allowed to use bad language. Anyone else using foul language would be benched immediately.

No swearing would be the new team policy and we would practice the policy right away. Anyone who felt the need to swear should raise his hand, one finger for English, two for Spanish, and the designated swearer would speak for him. I would be the designated swearer. The players looked at me, then at one another, smiled as if this were the craziest thing they had ever heard, and sprinted out to their positions. With fungo bat in hand, I began spraying balls all around the field. Ares flubbed a hot shot down the first baseline, immediately raising his hand, turning his back to home, hustling after the ball, his hand now raised awkwardly behind him, one finger pointed skyward. "Fuck," I yelled.

Ares fell, laughing. Everyone cracked up. After that every single player began to play harder, hustle more, and move livelier, players diving for balls, missing, raising their hands, the coach cursing into the wind, players at the bat, swinging, missing, raising their hands, the coach performing his designated duty, the din of laughter always in the background.

When the games began, the policy continued, except that the coach was a lot more discrete. A player would make an error, up would go the hand with pointed finger or fingers, and I would cover my mouth, gesturing to show I was doing my designated task. When we gathered between innings, I repeated, just for us, the swear word; there was a chuckle or two from the guys, and then down to business.

Interesting things began to happen. Right away umpires began to congratulate us on our sportsmanship. My guys began to scowl at the bad language used by opposing teams. We even began to play better—not great, but better. Our behavior got better—not great, but better. Teddy and Ares, the guys with the most talent, improved a bit, but continued to lead by bad example. Improvement in the classroom or on the ball field sometimes takes time and patience.

Teddy was such a fine athlete that he was recruited out of the eighth grade to play ball for a private high school in the area. The same antics he revealed to me got him kicked out of the private school, landing him with me. Even though I really had no idea how I was going to help him make better choices, I knew I would not dismiss him. Unwittingly, the system came to my rescue.

When a team had home field advantage playing on the city's premier field, there was a policy—the home team had to place a uniformed player on the other side of a cyclone fence that stretched behind the visitor's dugout down the first base line to retrieve any foul ball hit into that wooded area, rife with patches of poison ivy and strewn with urban litter. I wonder sometimes if educators who create such rules for kids have any children of their own. I also wonder if it is precisely these folk who contribute to the Teddys and Areses of public education, kids with attitude who show disdain for an absurd, impersonal system that champions sameness, compartmentalization, routine, and regulation. And so, some of our smartest and most gifted kids defy the service of a system whose metaphors emanate from the institutional handbook and the factory assembly line. Thus, they smoke during practice or relieve themselves in the middle of innings or use offensive language anywhere, anytime. Some pass school and graduate as part of the herd like boot camp survivors, learning never to volunteer or offer a thought or opinion. Many others drop out. We educational leaders delude ourselves into thinking that instituting programs or adopting a new textbook or a new set of standards or a tougher end-of-the-year exam will improve student learning. The Teddys of the world do not suffer us fools well, seeing the silliness for what it is, simply reacting with their own silliness.

They are McMurphy in the Cuckoo's Nest, fighting institutionalization, realizing the superficiality of a system that promotes standardization and mediocrity, and, too often, hypocrisy. Like McMurphy, they become outlaws against the system that quickly labels their behavior as irrational before they can expose the system for what it is.

While most of us are not outlaws, most of us really like outlaws. Maybe it is their soul, their spirit, their willingness to take risks, their rebelliousness—their disdain for the common, the mundane, the trivial, the inert. Randle Patrick McMurphy is the hero in Ken Kesey's novel, *One Flew Over the Cuckoo's Nest* (1963)—some say a Christ figure. Outlaw Randle Patrick McMurphy was lobotomized.

Thinkers and free spirits create institutional chaos. Smooth and safe and steady and secure, cries the institution in the face of ambiguity and chaos. Kill the spirit. Lobotomize the McMurphys. And school systems do.

* * *

I refused to be part of such a system, determining never to put a player into the poison ivy and syringe needles. The day before the game I bought dozens of baseballs, costing me more than what I was paid for coaching. The system had supplied me with but one dozen for the season. That is why we were ordered to place a uniformed player into the woods, to conserve the budget. So I bought my own baseballs, just as I bought my own pens and pencils and books for my English students.

At game time, the umpire ordered me to place my player in the woods. First, I attempted to explain why I would not. He was a dad. Attempting to use his sense of fatherhood to move him, I tried to tap into his imagination. Imagine a dad coming to watch his son play, being a bit disappointed he was not starting, but then not seeing him on the bench even, but sitting amid the urban blight and debris in foul territory. He didn't buy it. Folks who believe in the institution over the individual have no imagination. Institutionalization, I believe, eviscerates thought and compassion and empathy.

A rule is a rule; all the coaches in the city had agreed to it years ago. But can't you see, Ump, it's a bad rule. No matter. It is much easier to fall back on absolutes than to make moral decisions. He pointed in that umpire manner, and I thought he was going to throw me out of the game before the first pitch, when he snarled, "Play Ball," with the warning he would call the game as soon as I was out of baseballs. As fate would have it, more balls were hit into that first base foul area than anyone could remember. With each foul shot, the umpire grunted; I'd reach into my ball bag, pull out a shiny sphere, rub some dirt on it before tossing it gently to him. He'd glare, smirk, and place it into the bag. Another foul, another ball, another glare, another smirk. As the game went on, the fouls continued, so did the new balls. The glares grew, but the smirks diminished, making the glares more menacing. For sure, the next foul would end the game, read his face.

Inning after inning this game within a game went on, my kids watching, coach reaching into a bottomless bag, umpire angrily squeezing us on every close play, coach ignoring the inequities, kids observing, saying nothing. We lost, but we played differently that day, no silliness. Teddy controlled his bladder. The designated swearer remained mute.

"We lost a ton of baseballs, Coach."

"I don't care about the baseballs."

As I gathered the equipment to load into my van, I noticed every single player head for the woods on the other side of the cyclone fence, Teddy leading. I slowed my gait, fiddled with the equipment in the van, took my time changing my shoes, and watched in awe as uniforms scurried through the woods, bending over like potato farmers, their hands tossing aside Budweiser cans, brush, ivy, shopping carts, rags of clothing, syringes, all kinds of crap, finding many baseballs—some easily, others requiring a bit more digging. Ares had taken off his uniform top, using it as a ball bag. Others soon followed.

The harvest done, Teddy led the team back to my van, balls tied in shirts and gloves and hands. I barked at them, "You guys never listen to a thing I say."

Teddy countered, "How can we play for a coach with no balls?"

We began to win a few games; things were looking up until the day Ares was pitching a perfect game into the fifth inning, got up to bat in the last half of the inning, struck out, flung the bat, and uttered the magic word, forcing me to immediately call for a relief pitcher to start warming up. "Coach, I'm pitching a perfect game; I'm sorry about the swearing; it won't happen again."

When Ares threatened to leave the field and quit the team, I simply asked him to make sure he left behind his uniform. Ripping the buttons from top to bottom, he flung his uniform shirt at my feet, turned to go, hesitated a moment, nearly swore again, returned to the shirt, picked it up, shook out the dust, put it on, sat and steamed, holding his tongue and shirt closed. He was our best pitcher, our only real pitcher. I could taste that win, that perfect game; so could we all. For sure it was ours with Ares on the mound. The relief pitcher got bombed.

Later in the season we headed out to the suburbs to play against a private academy. City kids know they are different. "Hey, Coach, no Ricans out this way, right?" they asked, looking out at the countryside passing by. As soon as we got off the bus, we were met by the umpire.

"Coach, I want no bad language coming from your bunch." We simply stared at this guy as he walked away from us, wondering if he would address the other team this way. He didn't. In the fourth inning, when a ball went through the opposing team shortstop's legs, the angry pitcher loudly and clearly and unmistakably used the F-bomb. Later in the inning the pitcher once again cursed aloud. The umpire did nothing. In between innings I moseyed on over to the umpire as he strolled up the first base line.

"Hey, Ump, did you notice the vocabulary on that pitcher?"

"Yeah, Coach, I heard, but he didn't mean anything by it. It was harmless."

Screwing up all the self-control I could muster, squeezing my fungo bat to combat my temper, I calmly said, "Ump, my guys may look different from the kids you are used to. But they are kids too. When this game is over, you owe them a fucking apology." Turning, I walked back to my team, still squeezing my bat.

"Coach, we ain't never gonna get a call now," Ares said trying to mask a proud smile.

After the game, the umpire did come over to my team as we were debriefing. This is what I remember him saying: "Boys, I wanted to come over here to tell you that you taught me something about myself today." Fiddling with his mask as he moved it from hand to hand, he continued, "I live out here. Don't get to mix with city kids too often. Never thought I was prejudiced, but your coach, he got me thinking maybe I acted it." More fiddling with the mask, a bit of a step backwards, a cough, one hand holding onto the mask, the other covering his cough, then, "I apologize." Another cough, then, "Thanks for teaching me something about myself. Your coach is right—you guys play with class, a ton of class. Good luck the rest of the way."

The chatter on the bus home was different that day. Definitely, Ares knew he was something more than "a piece of shit." Definitely, I was even more convinced that winning has more to do than with the score at the end of the game.

I learned something else. Setting ideals, even in unorthodox ways, can lead to winning scores. It wasn't long before that baseball team began to win a series of city and state district championships.

*   *   *

Lessons from the baseball field translated into my English classroom. "Hey, Teach, when in the hell we gonna do English in here? All we do is read and write. I'm sick of this shit." It was Ares, in my English class where he sat right next to Teddy, and he bragged he had never read a book. He was not alone.

These kids had been placed in the lowest level classes throughout their schooling experiences. These low-tracked courses were designed for kids with the lowest levels of literacy to use curricular programs with worksheets. Indeed, the students in my low-level English class had *never* read a book or written a composition as part of their coursework. They had been placed in English classes in which they did not speak, did not write, and did not read. The curriculum was a teacher-proof program of computer print-outs scored by machines that required students to answer questions on SAT-like tests and to learn the basics of the five-paragraph essay. The goal was improved test scores, not improved literacy. The classes required students to be quiet, obedient, and task-oriented.

I wanted Ares and his classmates to believe in themselves as thinking and feeling human beings. I wanted to improve their confidence that they could perform real academic work. I wanted Ares and his classmates to understand that they, like the kids at Philips Exeter, had the ability to contemplate the good, the true, and the beautiful. I wanted Ares and his classmates to understand that language is magical because it can help us to celebrate what we were, what we are, and what we can become; because it can help us to see the complexity and beauty of our humanity; because it can help us to generate ideas; because it can help us to see with different eyes.

Our classroom would become a learning workshop, a language laboratory in which we would practice reading and writing every day around rigorous material. "Show me your mind thinking," I exhorted as we grappled with the literary outlaws such as Malcolm X, Holden Caulfield, Huck Finn, McMurphy, Antigone, Janie Crawford, and the like. Chaos reigned; resistance was the rule that first term as the unfamiliar approach unsettled us all. Thinking in English class was the unfamiliar. Reading in English class was the unfamiliar. Writing in English class was the unfamiliar. While a thinking curriculum may have been the norm for the kids at Philips Exeter, it was absent in low-tracked English classes.

Winning with my students meant getting them doing thinking that some believe can be done only in the highest-level classes or in the richest schools. By term two, I vowed, I would have the students in my class reading pieces of literature they had never seen before, grappling with meaning, and creating open-ended answers with panache and imagination. I expected the work of students in my low-level English class to be able to compete with the work produced by students in the AP courses. As on the baseball field, getting there would not be smooth. The high school policy was to issue failure warnings mid-term. That first term I announced, instead, I would issue passing warnings. I would pass anyone who completed a reading and writing portfolio, no matter how badly they had behaved or how poorly they had done during the term. Ares actually had gotten into the literature and seemed pretty animated in class, offering his opinions on the literature. The portfolio was set up such that most of the pieces were actually pieces we had worked on in class. I had seen Ares' working portfolio. He had everything done, and done better than most; however, he did not gather it together and did not pass it in. He flunked the term.

"How do I show my mind thinking?" Ares screamed in frustration one day at the start of the next term.

"You observe closely. You analyze carefully. You weigh the evidence. You predict a counterargument. Be unafraid to take a stand," I countered.

"What about the MCAS test?" he asked.

"You show me your mind thinking as you read and write and you'll beat that test."

I'll never forget the *Antigone* project. Ares and Teddy were to teach 5th graders to appreciate the tragedy of Sophocles. They rewrote the script "to help those little kids understand," arguing constantly over who was the tragic hero, Antigone or Creon. Each took his stand as competitors do, and each delved into the text to prove his argument. They went to the library, arming themselves with critics who could substantiate each person's claim. Finally, they decided to create a script that would entertain 5th graders and present evidence of elements of classical tragedy for each character and let the audience decide. To help 5th graders make an informed decision, Ares and Teddy broke down the definition of a tragic hero, complete with terms such as fate, hubris, and hamartia. Here is how they began their presentation:

"We're here this morning because we need your help. We have worked hard to present to you the play *Antigone,* a play having two main characters, Antigone and Creon. One of us thinks the tragic hero is Creon, the other thinks it is Antigone. We need you to help us resolve this problem. As you watch the play, observe the actions of the characters closely, analyze them carefully, and when you think you have the tragic hero, look with your other eye, and make a case for the other character as the tragic hero. Force yourself to pick as the tragic hero the one you think it is not. Be sure to use the evidence of the play to back you up. OK, let's have some fun."

The play was clever and entertaining and informative—and so very respectful of the 5th graders. If I were not then certain whether or not Teddy and Ares understood the classical concept of tragedy, I was pretty well convinced after Teddy wrote a paper entitled "Who is the Man Here?: Gender Conflict in Antigone" and Ares wrote a paper claiming the novel *The Natural* was much better than the movie because Roy Hobbes in the book, unlike the character in the film played by Robert Redford, succumbs to his hubris, striking out, suffering undo indignity, losing everything—just like Creon.

By the end of that term, both Ares and Teddy had clearly shown their minds thinking. They even helped fifth graders do the same. Yet on the last day of the term, Ares still had not passed in his portfolio. That day I stayed after school very late, so late that my car was the only one left in the lot. As I walked to it carrying my bag of portfolios, a hooded figure sat on the curb next to my car. No words were exchanged. I unlocked the door; he raised his hand offering me his portfolio. I took it; he got up from the curb and walked off.

3

Commentary on Coach McDermott's Narrative

Not-learning is a healthy though frequently dysfunctional response to racism, sexism, and other forms of bias. . . . Until we learn to distinguish not-learning from failure and respect the truth behind this massive rejection of schooling by students from poor and oppressed communities, it will not be possible to solve the major problems of education in the United States today. Risk-taking is at the heart of teaching well. That means that teachers will have to not-learn the ways of loyalty to the system and to speak out for, as the traditional African-American song goes, the concept that everyone has a right to the tree of life. We must give up looking at resistant students as failures and turn a critical eye towards this wealthy society and the schools that it supports.

— Herbert Kohl (1994, p. 32)

In her 2006 American Educational Research Association (AERA) presidential address, Ladson-Billings reminded us that too many researchers and policymakers focus on the *gaps* between poor and wealthy, Black and White, immigrant and non-immigrant. Framing the problem this way forces us to highlight micro-level interactions within families and between families and school. It leads theorists, educators, and activists to narrowly approach

Reflections From the Field, pages 21–27

the "problem of underachievement" by changing individual teachers or, more common and problematic, changing young people, their families, and/or cultures to close the gap.

Rather than view the gap (and, thus, individual teachers, families, youth or cultures) as the problem, Ladson-Billings urged us to identify the "historical, economic, sociopolitical, and moral decisions and policies" (2006, p. 5) as the foundation for the injustices that manifest in the "education debt" owed to Black and Brown, low income, and/or immigrant students. She argues that we need to redefine the problem as the larger forces of global capitalism and White supremacy and confront the immorality of a system designed to further oppress marginalized populations.

In "Teaching Toward Democracy: Educators as Agents of Change," Ayers, Kumashiro, Meiners, Quinn, and Stovall (2010) wrote, "[W]hile children and their families are the root of our concern, any honest and moral accounting of the lives of our students sweeps us immediately into the wider world and opens our eyes to the grinding effects of poverty" (pp. 12–13). Duncan-Andrade and Morrell (2008), building on the work of social reproduction theorists, contended that urban schools do exactly what they are designed to do; they manufacture failure on a large scale. To think that they do otherwise is to buy into the mythology surrounding the educational system, to believe that the institution of schooling provides opportunities for those willing to take advantage of it and those who do not succeed simply do not work hard enough to earn those benefits. The myths of educational opportunity and meritocracy lead to investments in stereotypical thinking about urban youth (that they, their families, or their cultures are deficient in ways that lead to school failure) and to blaming them for their own failure. Rather, schools are designed to reproduce social location, shoving urban youth into predetermined lower rungs while slotting White, middle/upper class youth into top positions on the social ladder (Bowles & Gintis, 1976).

James McDermott's narrative exposed the absurdity of an educational system designed to systematically manufacture the failure of youth of color, poor youth, and/or immigrant youth. As a coach and English teacher, McDermott acknowledged that he worked within this same system and attempted to find a role for himself that did not collude with the further oppression of youth. His literary heroes, rebels such as McMurphy, Janie Crawford, Antigone, Malcolm X, Huck Finn, and the like, provided one model for a possible role. Yet, he was all too aware of the fate they met for challenging convention and directly confronting oppressive structures; they ended up lobotomized, ostracized, dead.

Coach McDermott's narrative, then, is about an alternative response that an adult can play, a role that requires sacrifice but does not result in the fate of the rebel icons. He introduced a role that has the potential to create different outcomes for youth. He wrote about being an *ally* to oppressed youth and using his insight and creativity to protect his players' (and students') dignity against a dehumanizing educational system.

Ares and Teddy were not unlike the adolescents that Michelle Fine worked with for her acclaimed book, *Framing Dropouts* (1991). Fine found:

> [T]he dropout was an adolescent who scored as psychologically healthy. Critical of social and economic injustice, this student was willing to challenge an unfair grade and unwilling to conform mindlessly. In contrast, the student who remained in school was relatively depressed. Self-blaming, this student was more teacher dependent, unwilling to challenge a misgrade, and endlessly willing to conform. By the end of this research I worried about those who left public high school; but I also worried about what we instill in those who remain. (p. 4)

Like Fine, Coach McDermott was worried both about his students' investment in an institution that disrespects them and also worried about their rejection of it. To confront this paradox, he used his own power and creativity as a coach to protect his players' psychological health and affirm their refusal to conform, while simultaneously protecting their educational and social well-being by engaging in a rebellion that didn't jeopardize their standing as players or students.

Coach McDermott embodied a *pedagogy of trust* (DeMeulenaere, 2012), a pedagogy designed to counter the (understandable) distrust between marginalized families and schools over decades of mistreatment. In this chapter, we outline four characteristics of a pedagogy of trust that are exemplified in Coach McDermott's story: affirming students' realities, aligning with students against injustice, teacher risk-taking, and creative conflict.

Affirming Students' Resistance

A pedagogy of trust is grounded first and foremost in the lived realities of students. Coach McDermott exemplified this practice through his affirmation of his students' resistance to schooling. He never denigrated his players; he saw their antics as a logical response to a school that undermined their humanity. He affirmed their resistance even as he recognized that their modes of resistance would, in the end, not create more positive outcomes. Whether students cursed or smoked on the field, Coach McDermott saw these acts not as simply oppositional behavior, but as important acts of resistance. The school refused to take his players and students seriously, so his players and students refused to take the school seriously. This is how Fine's dropouts maintained their psychological health, by defying a system that called them "pieces of shit" (see Chapter 2). Of course, in their defiance, they reaffirmed the system's denigration of them. It was a no-win situation. They were Willis' lads (1981) who fought the system only to end up outside the school's gates without a diploma (though, on their own terms).

Furthering Giroux's (1983) theories of resistance, Coach McDermott viewed even small acts of defiance as forms of resistance. Even though these acts in the end became self-destructive, he didn't minimize the importance of the rebellion, but instead focused on the outcome. As Fine found, theirs was a psychological victory even if the outcome failed pragmatically. Coach McDermott argued that willful resistance to the majoritarian definitions of success (on the field and in the classroom) might very well be the most sane response to the insanity of a system that attempted to destroy their very souls. Kohl (1994) wrote, "To agree to learn from a stranger who does not respect your integrity causes a major loss of self. The only alternative is to not-learn and reject their world" (p. 6).

The students and athletes with whom Coach McDermott worked faced affronts to their integrity and identity regularly: spending ten years in school without acquiring basic literacy skills, being underfunded in the classroom and on the field, and, perhaps most egregious, having educators believe so little in their potential. Coach McDermott began his coaching experience by embracing the resistance as a "sane alternative" to an insane and dehumanizing system. But he embraced this in creative and unconventional ways, both on the field and in the classroom.

Aligning With Youth

Ayvazian defined an ally as follows:

> [An ally is] a member of a dominant group in our society who works to dismantle any form of oppression from which she or he receives the benefit. Allied behavior means taking personal responsibility for the changes we know are needed in our society, and so often ignore or leave to others to deal with. Allied behavior is intentional, overt, consistent activity that challenges prevailing patterns of oppression, makes privileges that are so often invisible visible, and facilitates the empowerment of persons targeted by oppression. (Ayvazian, 2007, p. 724)

Coach McDermott's working-class background from the same city aligned him with his students in some respects. However, he was also aware that he had privileges and access to power as a White college-educated adult that he could use on behalf of his players and students. This enabled him to, for example, purchase supplies for the classroom and buy a bottomless bag of baseballs. He also had the privilege to remain silent in the face of injustice, yet he chose to stand in solidarity to his students and players (for example, speaking directly to umpires on behalf of his players). As so few do, McDermott embraced "the proud and honorable role of ally: the opportunity to raise hell with others like us and to interrupt the cycle of oppression" and worked "to stir up good trouble, to challenge the status quo and to inspire real and lasting change" (Ayvazian, 2007, p. 725).

Adults in urban schools who recognize the dehumanizing forces of the school system have a choice. They can choose to be allies with oppressed youth as Coach McDermott did, or they can "collude, through their silence and inactivity with" oppression (Ayvazian, 2007, p. 726).

Risk-Taking

Allying with youth and affirming their defiance poses risks to educators such as Coach McDermott. These risks, though, cannot compare to the risks their youth face. Coach McDermott, aware of the risks to his players and students, welcomed the risks to himself, defying his principal's advice to not take Ares onto his team. He confronted umpires and refused to comply with rules that endangered and disrespected his players. The cost to him was nothing compared to what the players would have faced. So, instead, he intervened, knowing the risks to himself were minimal by comparison.

In taking the lead in resistance and embracing the risks, he also earned the trust of his players. We can see that when he walked back from telling off the umpire in the suburbs and Ares chimed in, "We ain't never gonna get a call now"—we can sense the pride displayed on Ares' face (see Chapter 2). What must it have meant to a young person who had spent so much of his energy fighting to have a coach join him in the fight? How many teachers and coaches see a critical aspect of their work as defending the humanity of their students? This is how trust is developed. This is why Teddy and Ares and the other players and students took Coach McDermott seriously.

Coach McDermott revealed that trust is built in classrooms and on fields when adults stand in solidarity with their students and players and, in the words of Kohl, "not-learn the ways of loyalty to the system" (1994). When such trust can be established, all the classroom management strategies become largely irrelevant. Trust comes when adults prove themselves allies.

Creatively Embracing Conflict

What Coach McDermott did so creatively was model for other adults how to challenge an oppressive system in ways that exposed the collusion as absurd. The foul balls scene was a great example. He tried to plead with the umpire who asked him to send a player into the garbage strewn woods to field stray balls. He asked the umpire to act differently in light of the danger the policy placed children in, standing among dirty syringes and urban pollution. When that didn't convince the umpire, he went for empathy as a father. That failed, too. Anticipating that his pleas would not change the umpire's mind, he had a plan that allowed him to follow the spirit of the rule; he made sure the umpire didn't run out of balls. For each stray ball, Coach McDermott pulled out a brand new ball. His players watched this drama unfold and, for them, each moment was creative resistance in the face of power.

What he modeled was not simply affirming the dignity of his players and protection of them from retribution for defiance. His actions revealed more than how to defy the system in a secretive and hidden manner that avoided harm. He found creative ways to use the system's rules to highlight the absurdity and dehumanization of the system. He confronted the suburban umpires' failure to take action about the suburban team's cursing not because he cared about the opposing team's cursing, but because he wanted to confront and challenge the bigotry of the umpire and the racism of the system. He not only chose to act in defiance of the system, but he acted in deliberate and creative ways to disrupt and expose the absurdity of the system. Rather than collude in silence or defy, his actions were calculated to pragmatically effect change.

Forging New Norms in Spaces of Trust

Coach McDermott serves as a model for other educators on how to implement a pedagogy of trust. This is not just the story of an adult ally cleverly helping youth thumb their noses at the system. He is more than an iconoclast working to destroy oppressive conditions; he also sought to build more humane ones. He was not against rules, expectations, and structure—just the ones that didn't make sense. Indeed, his field and dugout became spaces with guidelines and expectations, and he was anything but soft on his players and students. We see this when Ares was pitching a perfect game. Ares broke the established expectation of not cursing, and Coach McDermott pulled him, knowing it would cost them not only the game, but Ares' perfect pitching game. Coach McDermott was not dissuaded when his best pitcher threatened to walk.

In this scene, we gain further insight into how respect is earned. Ares and Teddy and the rest were not against structure and rules as the school's administration believed. They valued and respected rules and structures, when they knew what they meant and when they were in a space of trust. The small rebellions created by Ares and Teddy and many others in our urban schools are not simply a defiance of rules in general nor an eroding of the moral codes in our communities, as so many culture critics decry (Bennett, 1993; Bloom, 1988). Their defiance isn't a condemnation of rules or schooling; rather, it is an affirmation of their own dignity.

As the ending of Coach McDermott's narrative revealed, Teddy and Ares and the rest respected the rules on the field and in the classroom because they respected and trusted their coach and teacher; his actions proved that he was trustworthy. Indeed, their respect and trust for Coach McDermott was deepened because his structures and rules held his players and students to higher standards. He expected more from his players and students than other teachers and administrators did. Such rules and expectations in spaces of trust reflect the high regard of students and players. There is no absence of respect for rules and discipline among urban youth today; rather, there is a lack of earned trust in our schools and communities.

Like Coach Wooden, Coach McDermott's rules, mentorship, and role modeling were about nurturing young, powerful lives. He cared deeply about his players and students. He was thoughtful about working with them to create full and meaningful lives. This started with a deep belief in the potential of his students and players to lead lives that confronted oppression in ways that did not undermine themselves. It continued with his own actions to create spaces for them to succeed. It was made possible by the relationships that he nurtured with his students and players.

4

The Lie Is More Sinful Than the Score

Chad R. Malone
Premier Elite Athlete's Collegiate

Everyone in the Sullivan High gym knew the score. The scoreboard numbers read "90–6." The Highland Park Lady Cougars had just been humiliated—hold on, humiliated doesn't convey the slaughterhouse scene I witnessed that night on the basketball court. The Sullivan girls' basketball team laughed and high-fived through four quarters of a malicious bludgeoning. When they came out in a full court press, up 67 to 2 midway through the third quarter, I began to laugh, recognizing the scene for what it was: an absolute degradation of the Lady Cougars' spirit. A crushing of souls. It was the cruelest sporting moment I have ever witnessed.

Then, try to imagine my confusion when the athletic director from Sullivan pulled me aside as I had just made it out the door of the crime scene. He had already spoken to some of the girls and now he was telling me. "Those girls did a nice job. They handled themselves well considering the circumstances." I wasn't the coach, but I traveled with the team to their away games as a chaperone. I was invested as much as any committed fan. I don't know how, but I managed to edit the words that swirled in my mind down to a PG-rated, "You're joking, right?" and then followed my own advice to the girls, and "got on the damn bus before anyone (evidently including me) does anything stupid." With this athletic director in my face, surrounded by affluent parents scurrying their kids into SUV's, I could have easily done something stupid. I didn't. I got on the damn bus and we headed back to our school in Main South Worcester—a neighborhood as different from this suburban community as the two scores in the game.

When the Sullivan athletic director told them, "Nice game," on their way out, in an attempt to perform emotional triage after the massacre, it pissed me off. The players saw the scoreboard. They knew the score. This athletic director was lying. Well-intentioned lying, but lying nevertheless. And it was right there, in that yellow school bus, pressed in by the hideously uncomfortable brown bench seats, that I realized that the lie was more insulting than the score.

After witnessing the 90–6 loss, I volunteered to coach the Lady Cougars. It was my first head-coaching job, but I wasn't nervous. I was driven by strong purpose and clarity—to be honest with the players about the past and to create a new truth together going forward. At our first practice, I huddled them together and started with that truth.

"That was the worst loss I have ever seen. We were humiliated in the gym that night. Our school was humiliated in the paper the next morning. It was not right. It wasn't fair. It was messed up. So right now, we have a choice. We can spend the rest of the season blaming everyone for what happened. Yes, Sullivan ran up the score. That says something about them as a team and individuals. The bottom line is that the loss is ours and we need to own it."

During this time of brutal honesty with the basketball team, I began to reflect upon what I was doing in the classroom as an English teacher. With the help of that loss, I knew where we stood as a basketball team. But I wasn't so sure whether we were winning or losing in the classroom. It was at this time that I began to glean insights from the court that I would eventually carry into the classroom.

*   *   *

At the end of my third year of teaching, I was voted Teacher of the Year at my school. While the assistant principal helped me into the Teacher of the

Year jacket, I couldn't help but think what a load of crap it all was. I had students who had been sitting in my English class all year who couldn't read or write any better than when they first got there. Here I was, Teacher of the Year, with a jacket and a parking space; but, like the players walking out of the Sullivan gym that night, I knew the score. So even if my assistant principal and my colleagues told me, "Nice job," I knew better. The scoreboard glaring down on my classroom told the real score.

To be sure, my students were literate and "educated" according to the scoreboard kept by the district: students in my classes had moved their standardized test scores from "needs improvement" to "passing." They were not, though, doing the sophisticated type of writing and critical reading demanded from students in advanced placement courses; they were not prepared to do the work that would be demanded of them in college.

Yet, what I did with the students was "good enough" because they were performing a little better than they had before. Whatever I got the students to do was good enough for "those kids" who, according to most of the staff, were (at best) destined for the local community college. I was doing a good enough job. If my classes were basketball teams, we would have finished the season 6–14, just under the middle of the pack, in the worst league in town. And after the season was over, everyone would pat me on the back and say, "Nice job, coach. You should have seen how bad they were last year. They didn't win many games, but you are doing great." My mediocrity was mistaken for excellence.

It was during this same year that the Lady Cougars began to win and win big. Slowly, over time and with a lot of work, the young women, many of whom played on the 90–6 night, turned into a competitive basketball team. As I was being awarded Teacher of the Year, my team was headed to the school's first ever state tournament. I should have been on top of the world; but when I looked honestly at the work my students were doing in class, I knew that the lie prevailed.

What I learned about the importance of honesty in coaching had not yet carried over into my work as a teacher. In basketball practice, if a player failed to touch a line while running sprints, my response was automatic: "Do it again. Do it right. We will stay here all night if this is a problem for you." In the classroom, though, when students failed to touch a line, I applauded their lackluster work. The discrepancy between what I expected of my players and what I expected of my students was startling. If I was going to move forward as a teacher, I would have to be more honest with myself and with my students.

Students have sophisticated bullshit detectors. They know when their hands are short of the line. They also know what you mean when you congratulate that shortcoming with words like, "Nice work." Translation: "Nice work for a low-tracked kid no one expects to touch the line." And, as a first-year teacher concerned with being liked by students, the bullshit detectors created a cacophony of staggering proportions.

After a two-week unit teaching the basics of essay writing (leads, thesis statements, paragraph development, weaving textual evidence into writing, and generally trying to make sense of our thought with words on paper), a ninth grade student, Mark, turned in what could only be described as a jumbled hot mess about George's kindness in John Steinbeck's *Of Mice and Men*. I was so confused by his paper that I didn't know where to begin in grading it. I literally read his paper without making a single mark or comment and then left it lying unmarked on the kitchen table. The plot summary was interspersed with random thoughts about how nice George is. I couldn't find an argument.

I dove in for a second read searching for something nice to say or ideas I could begin to work with. I didn't want to hurt his feelings telling him what he probably already knew. I considered some final comments for Mark. "Your thinking is good, but we need to work on the structure of your essay." Or, "Mark, your sentences have good ideas, but you must be more clear." Ultimately, I left his paper blank. I had finally come to that moment on the school bus when I realized that the lie was more insulting than the truth. I had to be honest with Mark about his poor writing which meant I had to be honest with myself about my poor teaching.

The next morning, I went looking for him in the hallways before class.

"Hey, Mark." I handed him his paper. "Look at this, man. Wow. We really screwed up. I obviously don't know what the heck I am doing when it comes to teaching you and you don't know how to write an essay." I let it sink in. "What do you think we should do about this?"

Mark replied, "Uh . . . I don't know. I guess, fail me? I don't know. I don't really care anymore."

"That's garbage. If you didn't care, then you wouldn't have bothered to hand in anything."

Silence.

"So what are we going to do about this?" I repeated.

"Fix it?"

"Sure. We got a lot to fix, though. What are you doing right now?"

"Nothing."

"Let's fix it."

The hard work for both of us came with the follow through—making and taking the time to create an inspired essay that more closely reflected his thinking.

* * *

Being honest is not easy. It would have been a lot easier to write a few inane comments on Mark's paper than to sit down with him for countless hours until he understood. Honest words about the challenges facing a student or player without then providing the support to overcome those challenges, though, is just as cruel as the lie. Honesty enables us to understand our predicament, but we then need to figure out together a way through it.

My honesty with my team was a starting place, but we had work to do. A player can have all the heart in the world, but if the ability to pass, shoot, dribble, and play defense does not exist, then this player will be beaten to the hoop time and again, and the team she plays for will lose. Basketball is a game of skills that can be isolated, and the most fundamentally sound teams are the ones that win. Teams that know how to box-out, play great defense, and move the ball on offense, succeed. Teams that do not, lose. The majority of the girls I coached on that Lady Cougars team had very few technical skills. They had played in non-instructional recreational leagues meant to keep them busy, not teach the skills necessary to win games.

As I reflect upon how I teach basketball skills, I realize how clear my style is. For any individual skill, especially when building a technical foundation of know-how, such as taking a lay-up, there are "Yes" examples and "No" examples of how to execute the skill. Each drill targets a skill, then I provide clear "Yes, this is the right way to do it" examples for the girls to see, and then I give them "No" examples and all of this happens before the drill begins. When the girls go through the drills, they repeat the drill until their form matches the "Yes" example. The process is clear.

The students in my English classes had often come from non-instructional classrooms—they had been given work to keep them busy, not to improve their reading and writing skills. For the most part, the students I taught lacked the technical skills to represent their ideas adequately in the academic game. As a beginning teacher, I had a panicked response and tried to do everything at once. Rather than isolating skills and slowly putting them together, I threw everything at them. I hadn't broken down reading and writing in the way I had divided basketball into manageable parts. In time, I came to realize how important it was to isolate a skill and allow students to master it. Coaching basketball and seeing how to break down the facets of a game helped me boil down English into manageable skill sets that made sense to students.

One of the few skills I focused on with students was how to control a sentence of 40–60 words. The sentence is the basic unit of thought, and students had to learn how to write sentences that embraced the complexity of their thinking. My students did not lack the ideas, creativity, and ability to analyze. If they lacked anything at all it was the ability to capture that thinking in mainstream academic writing. The equivalent in basketball is when a player mentally wants to move through three defenders to get to the hoop, but lacks the technical skills to make a cross-over dribble, shift the ball from her right to left hand, and then execute a spin move to the hoop. Taken as a whole, the trip to the hoop is a complicated process, but each part of that move to the basket is an individual skill. We can practice cross-over dribbles, then spin moves, and so on. Once we have the different parts mastered, we can weave them together in any number of combinations. The players now have options. In the classroom, I imagined my students having a ball of thought in their hands and a desire to score; they simply needed the skills to get there.

To get my kids to master the art of generating sentences, I turned to Francis Christensen's (1963) "Generative Rhetoric of the Sentence" that stressed the value of teaching students how to write cumulative sentences. Cumulative sentences, sentences stemming from a base simple sentence that then "accumulates" details through various subordinate clauses and phrases, provided a vehicle for students to capture their thinking on paper. Within the structure of a cumulative sentence, I taught students individual skills. By writing cumulative sentences, they learned that every sentence has a simple subject and predicate. They learned how to use and control appositives, noun phrases, participial phrases, and so on. The end result was that students were able to write complex sentences with style. They found that by learning how to write cumulative sentences, they then had the "writing moves" to get to the basket and score. We spent several weeks practicing and further developing this skill. Building on the cumulative sentence, I similarly taught the skills of paragraph writing, essay writing, narrative writing, argumentation, and critical reading.. Those were the fundamentals I built on. Of course, each became more and more complex, and then we worked to weave them all together like the drive to the basket.

Like my basketball team, many students came to my class without fundamental reading and writing skills. Our classes, like basketball practices, were devoted to building skill sets. Time and experience helped narrow down the skill sets that I deemed most necessary for success when it came to reading, writing, and thinking. I knew that I taught most effectively in the classroom when I taught like a basketball coach, providing clear "yes" and "no" examples of the fundamental skills that I knew were necessary for students to "get it right." When I taught effectively, I was the obsessive basketball coach, making my students touch the line until they got it right and not relenting until they created a "yes" example of their own.

*   *   *

In my third year of coaching the Lady Cougars, we started getting "good," or so we thought. We were smashing teams in our league by 20 points. Our record was 10–1. However, we played in the smallest league in town and had lost sight of the fact that we were only winning against small teams in our low-level division. While in the back of our minds we knew our limits, we chose to ignore this reality and relished in our relative success.

Then the reality check came. Amidst the growing delusion about our ability came our game against St. Andrew's Academy, the Division 1 powerhouse I had asked to be put on our schedule. I prepared the girls for the mental challenge of facing a stronger opponent, reminding them to play the way they had been taught: together, tough, and with tenacity. And they did for the first four minutes of the game; but then the opposition's talent, size, and advanced technical skill began to chip away at their commitment to play up to their ability. First, we fell apart. Then, we turned on each other, reverting to selfish play. I watched them lose their composure as all we had struggled to learn together in the past three years seemed to vanish instantly.

I had purposefully scheduled this challenging game for two reasons. First, I wanted my team to gain some perspective—to honestly gauge their skills as individuals and as a team. Ironically, in our success, we had lost some of that truthfulness that had been so important to our rebirth. As well, I wanted my players to learn how to play their game even when challenged; those same skills, knowledge, and experience are necessary to chip away at the mighty giant of a fiercer opponent.

I brought this philosophy into my English classrooms as well. By the time my students reached the 11th and 12th grades, I required that they read college level texts. When I first got students in the 9th grade, I wanted them to read and read and read; so I introduced texts where the connection, relevance, and importance were obvious. As they advanced, it was important to introduce students to reading situations in which the relevance was not as readily apparent and thus the challenge was greater. It did not appear, initially, to be fun to read Machiavelli's *The Morals of the Prince* and Michel Foucault's *Discipline and Punish*; but they did and they ended up appreciating not only the challenge, but what they learned from engaging with the reading. I wanted my students to struggle through difficult texts, but I also wanted them to have access to the ideas embedded there that were also relevant to their lives.

When my students first encountered these difficult texts, they acted like the Lady Cougars against St. Andrew's Academy. They complained. They sulked. They threw their hands in the air, whining, "I don't get it." They abandoned the skills, knowledge, and experiences they learned reading other texts—the very same skills that would have helped them chip away at the more complicated texts. Both my students and players got so used to winning coming easily that they forgot that larger challenges always loom. I wanted my students to read difficult texts, extracting information, because that was a skill needed to succeed at the next level of their education. I wanted them to persevere through challenge without losing their cool.

There wasn't much to say to the team immediately after the St. Andrew's Academy game. Players were too upset and angry to listen to anything. St. Andrew's Academy presented a reality that shattered their swagger. We ran into a team that was better, bigger, and badder than we were, and we lost our cool.

Like my students reading Foucault for the first time, they had forgotten that even the hard challenges should be approached in the same manner we approached games we knew we could win. In practice the next day, when the girls were calmer, I spoke about the basics—not letting another team take us out of our game plan, the importance of relying on what we had practiced, and, most importantly, keeping a clear mind and a sense of togetherness, regardless of the challenge. The morning after my students were to have to read a section of Foucault, I had a similar talk with them. I told them to attack difficult texts using the same principles they had learned with the easier ones. Slow down. Work with the parts you understand; then work your way out. Get the pen in hand. And keep frustration at bay.

I wanted my students and players to meet with wonderful success. Yet I also needed to keep a sense of honesty attached to our success. To do this, we needed to take on seemingly impossible challenges and allow ourselves to learn from our losses, so we could begin to win.

*   *   *

My tenure as the coach of the Lady Cougars ended where it started—with a big loss. In my fourth year as the coach, we made it to the semifinal game of the district tournament. It was further than any team of any sport had gotten in our school's history. We were annihilated in this game. We didn't really have a shot against the school. But the Lady Cougars never quit. They played their game, and they played it with heart. It was admirable; I was proud of the girls and I told them that. But, the post-game talk didn't end there. Right there in the locker room, with my players in tears, I asked them to remember this pain and to carry it with them into the next season.

"I guess I am supposed to tell you that you did okay and that really, you had already won before you took the floor today. In a way, you did. But the reality is that we lost.

"Do you feel it in your stomach? It hurts, right? That is what losing should feel like. When I first started coaching this team four years ago, you had gotten used to losing. The sting of loss was dulled. Now you feel it. I never want you to be okay with losing. It should hurt. It should feel like it does right now. And I want you to hate this feeling with all your heart for the rest of your lives."

I went on, "Any time you feel like this in your life, I want you to fight against it with everything you have in your soul. I want you to look at this loss and figure out what you need to do to win the next time you meet this team in this same gym next year."

*   *   *

It is very difficult to recreate the intensity of a post-game locker room in the classroom. Nonetheless, loss is a part of life, and we have to prepare youth for it. My students have received news that they failed the state standardized test that they are required to pass in order to graduate. My students have come up absurdly short of the SAT score the college of their dreams required for admission. My students have received rejection letters from colleges. My advice to them was the same as what I told my players. Losing is not okay. Learn from it, but never accept it. The teacher has taken lessons from the coach in finding ways to frame loss for kids who had become accustomed to it.

I find that so many educators are willing to accept losses for the kids they teach. Even worse, adults are willing to tell kids they are doing "fine" when the scoreboard, obvious to everyone, clearly states the opposite. Years later, I am still angry at the athletic director who told the Lady Cougars that they did "a nice job" after losing 90–6. It was a mean lie.

In my time as a teacher, I have tried not to lie to myself or my students. It makes my job more difficult and painful. My truth is that I have been an improving coach for longer than I have been an improving teacher. Truthfully, I was afraid of not being "loved" by students if I was as forceful in the classroom as I was as a basketball coach. I was afraid that the basketball version of me wouldn't fly in classroom.

My players know that I have too much respect for them to tell them a bunch of lies. They trust me to be honest because they know how much I care about them and love them. Through practices, team dinners, fundraisers, and hours on bus rides, we develop a trust and love that enables me to be unflinchingly honest with them. Always. And they are honest with me. Eventually, our honesty with each other spreads beyond hoops and into our everyday lives. Our trust and love transcends basketball. All of this comes naturally to me on the basketball court. Educational theorists call this developing "community" and "culture." I am just trying to build winning basketball teams and winning classrooms.

5

Commentary on Coach Malone's Narrative

Coach Malone's brave narrative of the ways his basketball coaching informed his teaching exposes and speaks to the culture of fear in which we live and teach our young. He intimately revealed that our efforts to protect young people from painful realities rarely provide any protection. Instead, the youth in his narrative knew when they were failing. But deception prevents dealing with present reality and authentically helping young people achieve a different future. We, as educators, are not only lying to the young people, but as Coach Malone revealed, we are lying to ourselves. Moreover, such obvious deception to young people fosters a distrust that undermines the classroom culture necessary for learning.

Perhaps it is also a fear about not knowing how to help youth improve that paralyzes us as educators. Coach Malone admitted that he was unsure

Reflections From the Field, pages 39–44

how to help his student, Mark, analyze *Of Mice and Men*, capture his budding ideas, and teach him the writing skills requisite to communicating those ideas eloquently in an essay.

Maybe it is not simply about fear; maybe it is just as much about laziness. To borrow from James McDermott's piece in this volume (see Chapter 2), maybe the students are fake reading and the teachers are fake teaching, and everyone knows it and continues with the charade because no one wants to put in the time and energy needed to look at this unmistakable truth squarely and deal with it.

Coach Malone's narrative gives us an insider's view of how one coach confronted these fears and put in the necessary time and energy to create a winning team and support a college-bound environment in his classroom. He used very distinct tactics. Specifically, he used direct, explicit instruction with his players and students, drew on learning theory to encode important information, and focused his players' and students' learning on a few fundamental elements of basketball and English.

Direct, Explicit Instruction

In this culture of fear, educators are often afraid to not only tell youth that they are not doing something correctly, but to give them the rules necessary to win at the academic game. Indeed, Lisa Delpit called this the "silenced dialogue" (Delpit, 1988). Delpit showed how educators, primarily White and middle class, frequently feel uncomfortable by obvious displays of power such as that made most tangible in direct speech. She found that these teachers instead tend to use indirect verbal communication to lessen the visibility of the differentials of power. However, students, particularly those who are unfamiliar with the "culture of power" (Black and Brown, low income and/or immigrant youth) are confused by this indirect speech and are unable to improve their writing when explicit instruction in writing is not given. How much is the delusion that everything is okay in classrooms and gyms a result of the educators from spaces of power and privilege trying to minimize their own guilt? How much of the failure of students of color can be explained by teachers afraid to be uncomfortable and confront their race and class privilege?

Delpit's framework, eloquently captured in Coach Malone's narrative, revealed that when teachers, operating from the culture of power, encounter individuals who lack the knowledge of the codes, skills, or practices of that culture of power, they must explicitly teach those codes, skills, and practices. When we fear acknowledging that players and students are not succeeding and, instead, resort to lying to them and/or relegating them to low-tracked classrooms, we fail to do our job as educators to teach. When we are afraid to teach students the codes, skills, and practices they need to succeed, we fail to educate.

Coach Malone argued that these lies might be well-intentioned. However, they do not benefit the students or players; they benefit those with power and privilege. Whether they prevent people in power from engaging in the necessary hard work with honesty or simply protect them from the discomfort of having to confront their own privilege, the gain is all accrued to those with the most power—not the students.

Of course, when and if teachers are able to honestly confront the discrepancy, they then must follow through to address the challenge. Coach Malone explicitly used direct instruction to teach the missing skills, codes, and practices. He, echoing Delpit, reclaimed the pedagogical viability of explicit instruction. It was not at the exclusion of more progressive pedagogies. Even within a critical or constructivist teaching paradigm, there are times when direct instruction is needed. Even Freire conceded this when he became head of education in Sao Paulō (Freire, 1993). No one would ever expect to learn to drive a car without direct instruction about gas and brake pedals, gears, and the dashboard. While direct instruction helps, the driving student must also construct understanding through experience and practice releasing a clutch to begin acceleration. Such pedagogies are not in opposition; they are based on the type of learning required.

Concept Attainment, Automaticity and Focus

When Coach Malone began to think about explicit instruction, his framing of both coaching and teaching connected directly with many insights from cognitive learning theory. Most clearly, Malone's teaching of basketball skills and writing and reading skills drew on the curricular strategy of concept attainment (Johnson, Carlson, Kastl, & Kastl, 1992), which was developed from Jerome Bruner's (1996) theories of conceptual learning. Malone's presentation of "yes" models and "no" models in a piece of writing or on a basketball floor represented a simplified account of what amounts to a complex process. In this two-stage process in which the teacher or coach models both positive and negative exemplars, students construct a sophisticated understanding of the concept. Indeed, concept attainment makes the seemingly simple concepts more complicated and nuanced, which enables students to develop a sophisticated understanding they can then transfer to other contexts.

Take for instance the cross-over dribble. Is it simply shifting the dribbling from one hand to the other? What about the motion of the dribbler's body? Does that shift in the process or not? If the shift in dribble occurs through the dribbler's legs or behind the back is that still a cross-over dribble? Concept attainment helps to determine the boundaries of the concepts. It also helps the learner determine the purpose and use of the concept. This level of sophisticated understanding is important so that students understand how to reproduce this knowledge in varied contexts. This, of course, is similar to the "sandwich model" that Coach Wooden employed (see Chapter 1).

It also helps teachers assess student comprehension. In the second phase of concept attainment, students apply the concept in different contexts. It is here that educators begin to see if students understand the concept and can apply it. This is also where we can clarify misunderstandings. Too often coaches and teachers fail to account for misunderstandings and address them. The task of an effective coach is to not only identify the mistakes made, but also to trace them to their conceptual base so that understanding can be clarified.

Figuring out the concept and its use is critical. So, too, is committing certain skills to long-term memory (Eggen & Kauchak, 2001). Indeed, as coaches teaching specific skills, we want to make these skills automatic. Once the concept is understood in a way that is organized and purposeful, there needs to be practice to achieve automaticity. And that practice needs to continue to develop in sophistication. No player can hope to make a cross-over dribble and spin move around several players on the way to the hoop without first having practiced to the point of automaticity the basics of dribbling (Bruning, Schraw, & Ronning, 1999). Coach Malone's narrative reclaimed the value of practice.

He also realized that for his team to be competitive, his players needed to be great at a few fundamentals. Indeed, he emphasized the mastery of a few key fundamentals in basketball and English over a wide breadth of knowledge that lacked depth. Rather than develop a cursory understanding of all aspects of basketball, his players focused on key skills and concepts. Similarly, he had six basic elements he wanted his students to understand as students of English. The reason to focus on these six basic elements was not to simplify the course, but rather to foster a masterful level of learning. That mastery could then be further developed by providing different contexts in which to present or refine these skills; any extension on these elements was not new, but rather the same elements offered in a different context. These basic elements were a vehicle for expressing ideas; students could better attend to their ideas because they were not bogged down in an endless number of seemingly disconnected grammatical rules.

Engineering Failure

When his players first confronted an opponent that was stronger, faster, and more experienced, they lost their composure and could not figure out how to translate their skills into this new, more challenging context. Similarly, his students forgot how to apply their analytical skills when faced with more challenging texts and how to apply the six basic elements when given more complex writing assignments. This experience was engineered by Coach Malone; he knew they had enough confidence to successfully navigate small bodies of water in which they were big fish. He wanted them to also learn to face sharks in oceans without losing their composure; he wanted them to learn that their skills and abilities would, if they kept their composure and focused on what they did well, make them competitive at any level.

Carol Dweck's (2006) theory of learning offers great insight into framing Coach Malone's goals for his players and students. Through her research, Dweck determined that there are two different types of mindsets: fixed and growth. The fixed mindset attributes success to natural talent and abilities and views success as affirmation of those existing talents. When faced with new challenges in a different context that they do not already know how to work through, individuals with a fixed mindset give up, arguing that they are simply not "good enough."

By contrast, the growth mindset sees talent as a starting place, but believes that capability is developed through effort and perseverance. Students with a growth mindset, who meet with a challenge that is beyond their present abilities, continue to work hard to figure out how to "win." They come to believe that it is their effort that is their strength. They attribute failures to the need to try harder. The fixed mindset attributes the same failures to a natural lack of ability to complete the task.

Turning back to Coach Malone's work with his students and players, his decision to place difficult challenges in the paths of the youth with whom he worked was an effort to help them develop a growth mindset. For youth who had been told repeatedly that they were not smart or not talented (through subtle practices such as tracking), they held tight to a fixed mindset—one that told them that they were naturally not smart and untalented. Coach Malone encouraged them to adopt a growth mindset, one that told them that they could achieve anything they put their minds to if they worked hard, maintained their composure, applied the skills and knowledge they had, and remained determined.

The primary attribute of the fixed mindset is that a specific event defines an essential characteristic and, thus, determines an identity. The 90–6 defeat of the Lady Cougars confirmed the team as "losers" with the fixed mindset. The growth mindset does not link individual outcomes to core aspects of one's identity. Instead, a loss (or win) becomes a means to figure out what to change. Each experience is a tool for growth. Challenges and failures are embraced as spaces of learning.

Beyond developing the skills and conceptual understandings, what Coach Malone did exceptionally well as a coach and teacher was encourage a growth mindset in his players and students. He taught students to believe that hard work, more than innate talent, is the path to success. Failure was embraced as a place for learning. Coach Malone used failure, even orchestrated it, as a way for students to confront their fixed mindset and push them into a growth mindset.

And in his final speech he did not minimize the importance of failure. He asked them to embrace it and feel the pain of it. He said, "I want you to look at this loss and figure out what you need to do to win the next time you meet this team in this same gym next year" (see Chapter 4). He pushed his players to look honestly at loss to figure out their next steps in the journey to success. This type of honesty requires courage and embraces failure as part of that journey.

6

Learning to Detrack on the Volleyball Court

Colette N. Cann
Vassar College

After graduating college, I coached a high school volleyball team in California's Central Valley. The Central Valley landscape is dotted by farms as much as it is by family restaurants, malls, and movie theaters. It was, at that time, a rural community making room for mid-level dot-commers looking for affordable housing and suburban-like public schools. From my home, I could drive in any of three directions and be sitting in a brown and orange booth eating a burger and fries in under five minutes. Drive a few minutes further and I would pass trailer homes on small farms whose tenants struggled with the unexpectedly early warm weather that year. A little further, perfectly aligned rows of trees would flit past my car window indicating the large commercial farms that grew the nation's almonds.

Reflections From the Field, pages 45–54

The town and high school seemed to be comprised of mostly White families; however, the census recorded a significant Latino population. There were very few Black families in town; there were none on the volleyball team I coached and I never met any Black students at the high school where I coached. Yet as a Black girl raised in Los Angeles playing volleyball, this was not new to me. I rarely saw other Black players in my leagues and, only once, had another Black player on my club season team. Volleyball, at that time, was a "White" sport. I had played varsity volleyball throughout high school and tournament volleyball in college. Growing up in southern California, I had learned volleyball in elementary school and played competitive volleyball starting in the seventh grade. Volleyball in southern California can only be competitive, played year-round with no off-season.

As such, race undoubtedly acts as a thick smoke curling around the words of this narrative. All of the players I coached (and the coaching staff with whom I worked) are White. The lessons learned on the volleyball court, though, I took into both primarily White private schools as well as urban, primarily Black and Brown schools when I began my teaching career. Lessons about the necessity of community and how to build it among youth, lessons I learned as a coach, are critical to classroom teaching, as is acknowledging the integral role every player and student plays to win on the court and in the academic game.

* * *

In this predominantly White, suburban high school volleyball program, I was head coach of the junior varsity team (and assistant coach of the varsity team). Not a player who came out for preseason conditioning measured over 5' 9" nor cleared much more than her fingers over the net. They were kind, goofy, and cordial to a fault. They ran, stretched, and got a drink of water when asked. There were no superstars, but most of the players had enough of a foundation that they could improve into solid volleyball players. However, they lacked the aggressiveness of players who expect to win. For most of the players, volleyball was their second sport played "out of season" for their first sport, usually softball. They were disciplined athletes who looked to volleyball to stay in shape, but not to be competitive. We wouldn't win any games without increasing their aggressiveness.

So I increased the intensity of the drills. I hit the ball hard—never harder than I thought they could reasonably receive it; but I rarely gave them ones I knew they could pass easily. I hit the ball in hard-to-reach spots and yelled for them to touch it at all costs.

"Ready? Are . . . you . . . ready? You don't look ready. Ready is a state of mind. Ready is an attitude. Get low! Lower. If you don't get low you're not going to make it out of this drill. You have to earn your way out. It takes more energy to stand up and sit down than to stay down."

Whack! I hit the ball. It flew past the first player in the drill.

"You're not down."

Whack.

"Look. You're in this drill until you can get down."

Whack.

"Arms out no matter how tired you get. Get tough!"

Whack.

"What are y'all on the sidelines doing? Watching? Y'all have two options. If you're not shagging the ball, then you're cheering her on to get out of this drill. She doesn't get out of this drill until she looks like she wants more."

Whack.

"Are you getting tired?"

Whack.

"No matter how tired you are, you have to *want* the ball. You *want* the hitter to hit it to you and to hit it as hard as she can. You don't look like you want it!"

Whack.

"I'm out of balls! How am I out of balls? Everybody down for push-ups including me! She's still in this drill. Y'all better get it together and help her get out of this drill."

After the first week of conditioning, sore and bedraggled, the girls started getting tougher. They began asking for the ball, "Hit me, Coach! Hit me!" They asked to repeat the drill if they didn't think they got it right. For every player in a drill, there were at least ten girls shouting for her to "beat Coach"—to stay in it until *Coach* was too tired to hit anymore balls at her. We still had a long way to go, though. I knew I could teach the skills, and they had already begun to rise to the aggressive challenge. But we had no super stars who could carry the team even if we could get the ball to them.

As we moved into the season, I began to think about the players and their individual strengths. I assessed them based on their aggressiveness, motivation, skills in various positions, relationships with other players, and tendencies toward leadership. I called meetings with each player to set individual goals, hear her own thoughts on her growing strengths, and understand what she wanted her role on the team to be. With these data in hand, I began to formulate a strategy for coaching this team, one that depended on players' deep trust and knowledge of each other. We were not a team that was going to win based on power. We did not have the height nor the strength of other teams in the league. And we had no star volleyball players who could dominate a play. But each individual player had a set of core strengths that, when put together with the strengths of other players, made a competitive team.

I created a team of what I call *necessary dependencies*. Each player on the court was integral at that moment for other players to be successful in getting the point or the side-out. Each rotation required a configuration on the court that was specific to the rotation and the players on the court at the time. Trusting each player on the court meant trusting that each person uniquely filled her role. There was no such thing as the strongest player on the team, but the strongest player for that role in that play.

Their ability to read each other as well as the court became important within this context. Very few of the players were initially friends outside of volleyball; so I created opportunities for them to be together in other ways to get to know each other. For example, I required players to come to study table for an hour prior to practice to work on their homework together. This served the multiple purposes of them spending time together in a different way, forming identities as student-athletes, and working together to take responsibility for each other's well-being in other contexts.

The season unfolded favorably for the junior varsity team. For the first time in many years, the team had a winning record that drew parents and fans to the stands—and this was junior varsity! While we missed going to finals by one game, it was a significant accomplishment by novice players in a novice program.

* * *

During the club season that immediately followed the high school season (this was California, after all), I was hired to coach the top club team—a team that included two star players. The two star players were two-sport athletes who had already received college scholarships for the following year. They didn't show up for tryouts, but were accepted onto the team based on their reputations as players. The other players on the team knew about the two star athletes; they were excited to be on a team with the two, but also wary of how much playing time they'd get. I, too, was both excited and wary.

Not only could they clear the net, but, once they got the ball, they had the skills and experience to get the point or side-out. On the other hand, I was nervous because we started off the season without them even trying out. In fact, they were excused from most practices by the club manager because they played other sports for their schools. The club policy was that players were allowed to miss practices and games without penalty (without being benched) to play or practice for a school sport.

So the two players didn't practice with the team often, but were allowed to play in every game. Without them at practice, the others players were required to move around cones that stood in for the absent star players. Of course the cones were no substitute and, in games, chaos reigned. There is so much more to placement on the court than the agreed-upon play. Players intuitively respond differently and adjust in necessary ways even within the tightest of plays.

More importantly, the identities of the two players as stars created a *response identity* in the other players as "non-stars" who were only necessary to fill out the court. This was reinforced by the fact that they touched the ball once for every five times the two star players touched the ball. The two stars ran around the court touching balls that weren't even theirs—often out of position to touch the ball twice before it was sent back over the net. They became more sure of their identities as star players even as the team lost more and more games.

Eventually, losing game after game, the two players left the team. Our team wasn't winning, and the sacrifice was no longer worthwhile. But the other players who had been coming regularly to practices and games continued to play on the team. It was then that I was reminded of coaching with attention toward each player and creating necessary dependencies that lead to a greater whole. Winning is a task only accomplished with the strengths and skills of every player on the court. I wish I could say we then won every game; we didn't. We played harder, improved, and got in sync with each other. If we had started here at the beginning of the club season, there is no telling where we might have ended.

I failed as a coach during the club season because I failed to create a space where each player was integral to the identity of the team as a whole. Status differences among players were exacerbated by participation on the team rather than diminished. Our team did not serve to raise the level of every player's performance.

* * *

After my first year of graduate school, I took a position at an urban middle school that had had a string of substitutes all year. I was hired to teach pre-algebra to a group of eighth grade students for the last six weeks of school. One of the students in the class had been demoted from the upper track geometry class. Some were repeating this course from the previous year. Even with this heterogeneity, it was perceived as a low-tracked classroom with no "star" students.

The students in this class were much like my volleyball players on the first day of conditioning—they were missing the requisite aggressiveness necessary to win at the academic game. They were sweet, pleasant, and cordial (unlike, perhaps, our media images of them); but they seemed resigned to their losing streak.

Before I had a chance to do or say more than introductions, a Black female student cut to the thick of it: "You here to teach us the same old shit? Fractions are tired."

"No, I'm not here to teach you fractions. Have you been learning about fractions all year?"

"The other teachers think we don't know enough math to do anything but fractions. And they think we can't even do them. We been doing fractions since I got here."

Another student cut in, "You only got in this class in November. We been doing fractions longer than that."

"No one's going to be doing any fractions unless there are fractions in an equation. We're going to do some algebra and get you ready for the ninth grade," I replied.

"Real algebra?" asked the first girl. "Not some fake 'algebra for stupid kids' stuff, right?"

"Umm, right. Why would I ask you to do fake algebra?"

"Because, you know, the other teachers think we're too dumb to do real algebra. You think we don't know why we're in this class? Them kids over there," she continued pointing at the classroom next door, "aren't smarter than us because they White. I could be in geometry. I WAS in geometry. But I left because they kept looking at me funny and acting like I shouldn't be there. I was the only Black kid in there,"

"What's your name?" I asked.

"Dominique."

"Ok, Dominique, let's get straight on this right now. I know for a fact that y'all can do algebra. You can do geometry. It's not impossible, but it is pretty hard to do it without a teacher—the *same* teacher—all year long."

"She ain't lyin'. Every fool that's been through here gives us a test to see how much we know and then says we don't know math and teaches us fractions all over again," a young man said. When he'd come in the room, he had picked a seat in the middle of the desks I'd arranged in a semi-circle. He'd then slid all the way down in it with his baseball cap low over his face. He was now sitting up and had swung the rim of the cap to the side over his ear.

"I don't think we need to call anybody a fool," I said, smiling. "But I get what you're saying and I think you get my point. So, let's talk about this. You tell me that the kids over there are mostly White and I can see that the kids over here are mostly Black and Latino. They got a teacher all year and you didn't. They're in the advanced class and you're not. Dominique already said it doesn't have anything to do with anybody being smarter than anyone else. So, then what's it about? I mean, let's be real, they could have assigned that teacher to your classroom all year and given the geometry students the substitute teachers all year, right?"

"I think it's because everybody's racist. Ain't nobody White up in here. And ain't nobody Black or Mexican up in there. My name's Miguel by the way in case you wanted to know."

"Hmm, okay. So let's talk about that. How many of you think racism is to blame?" I asked.

Every hand in the classroom went up except Dominique's. "Dominique, what are you thinking?"

"Well, I think it's easy to say 'racism.' Nobody called me any names or really even said anything to me. I mean some students said they were surprised I was in there, but they were glad I was there. Nobody was in my face about it. And Mr. Johnson was excited when I said I wanted to take the class. He said he believed in me. So I don't know if I think everybody's racist."

"Well, let me ask you this? Can someone be racist or can we call something racist even when that person didn't intend it to be racist? Is it racism if everyone in this room is Black or Latino and everyone in that room is White?" I asked. I was genuinely interested in how they made sense of this.

"Those students are in there because they can do math and most of us except Dominique can't do math. If we could, we'd be up in that class. Ain't nobody racist." A voice of meritocratic reason chimed in right when I thought the conversation was going to be a little too smooth.

"What's your name?"

"Charlie and I know for real that I can't do math. This is my second time in this class and I'm still going to fail it. That ain't got anything to do with being Black. That's me not knowing the answers."

"Yeah, but you didn't have nobody teaching you all year, Charlie. What if somebody had been in here really teaching you?" Dominique inquired. She was sitting on the edge of her seat, almost standing now. It was as if only she and Charlie were in the room. She was so intent on him that he looked away uncomfortably.

"I... I don't know. I'm used to not being good at stuff. Maybe, I guess," he muttered.

Miguel cut in. "I been thinking about what you asked. Yeah, I think something can be racist without anybody doing it on purpose—without anybody being racist on purpose. I think it is racist because they have what they need and we don't and all of them happen to be one race and we all happen to be something different. Maybe nobody meant it like that. And maybe none of us in here except for her could pass that class anyway. But we can't take that class because we ain't never had any good teachers who think we can do anything other than add fractions—and they don't think we can even do that. So, yeah, I think its racism."

"Some folks might call that 'institutional racism' when it turns out that way. It doesn't have to do with any single person being a racist person so much so as the school system creating racist outcomes like what happened here this year. So, let me take a second to let you know what we're going to do about it.

"This is going to be one of the hardest classes you've ever taken, but hopefully not the hardest you'll ever take. We are going to try to do a year's worth of algebra in six weeks. You can't be absent, you can't be late, you can't decide you don't feel like working one day. Every single day, you have to be on it. In return, I'm going to be prepared. I made you algebra books that you can take home and work in. I have pencils that I am going to require that you use. My phone number is at the front of the book—call me in the afternoon if you get stuck on your homework. If you don't understand something, that's my fault. I didn't teach it to you well enough. But if you don't ask a question, that's on you. This is your class and you have to demand that you understand." And with that, we were off.

Desks were arranged in a large horseshoe shape around a table with six chairs in the middle of the room. I used the first 10 minutes of class for direct instruction that was as much about improving their note-taking skills for a high school mathematics class as it was about addressing mathematical concepts. I would then call up five or six students to the large table; I chose the students based on common areas that needed more instruction, so the groupings changed frequently. I worked with each of these smaller groups of students for 5–10 minutes. The rest of the class, when they were not at the table with me, worked either individually or collaboratively—but with explicit guidelines.

The norm guiding their independent work was that it was a student-monitored space. Students could ask help from any other student in the room and that student, no matter what she was in the middle of doing, had to put her pencil down and help the other student. No student providing assistance could put her pencil on the other person's paper, nor touch it in any way. The "tutor" had to use words and allow the other person to struggle through the problem. The test of whether the tutor had done a good job helping was that the person should be able to explain back to her what needed to be done.

I strategically worked to avoid having the star mathematics students be the ones on whom everyone else depended. I publicly praised students frequently about what they had to offer other students. This praise was given equally for their depth of knowledge as for their ability to teach for comprehension and their supportive language with other students.

This class work was framed within a rhetoric of community: As a community, we cared for each other and took responsibility for each other's academic well-being as well as our own. It provided opportunities for us to talk about the context surrounding the class, the program, tracking, and race. This classroom space and culture invited such conversations.

Three weeks into the work, Charlie, the student so used to "not being good at stuff" was frustrated with a problem. He slammed his pencil on the desk, got up and walked quickly toward the door with his head down.

Dominique, who had emerged as an advocate for the students in the classroom, asked him where he was going. "I don't get this stuff. Any of it. I been trying and it don't make no sense."

"That's not true. You explained the first problem to me earlier."

"You know what I mean. I can't get the harder stuff. I keep getting stuck," he cried out. He was struggling to hold tears back and I was afraid that he was going to lose that battle before he made it out the door.

"The lady said to tell her if you don't get it because then she'll explain it again. It's on you if you walk out the door." He had already made it to the door, but he hadn't opened it yet. He stood there while we all watched.

Dominique's voice got softer. "Come on, Charlie. If she can't explain it to you, I will. Please stay here." And with that, he walked back across the room, avoiding eye contact with everyone. Dominique got up, crossed the room and leaned over his desk. He didn't look at her, but he picked up his pencil and stared at his paper with tears in his eyes.

Every student except Charlie completed the work by the second to last day of the semester. Charlie had stopped coming to class shortly after the incident with Dominique. So on the last day of class, we had a somewhat muted celebration for passing this hurdle in their mathematics careers. It wasn't the same without him there.

To celebrate, I brought in a strategy game I had learned in Botswana. We were asked to use the geometry room next door because the school needed our classroom for testing. The geometry students were gone for the day, testing for courses they wanted to take in high school. The geometry teacher had an unexpectedly free period and was working at his desk in the room. Half an hour into playing the game, the geometry teacher pulled me aside to ask what magic I had worked on the pre-algebra class.

"I haven't heard anything through the wall since you got here. And here they are playing a game and no one's cursing or yelling or fighting. What'd you do?"

The assistant principal had asked me the same question a few weeks earlier. He called me out into the hallway during the class period and asked what was happening in the room. Confused, I had asked what he meant. "You haven't sent anybody down to my office for discipline. In fact, I haven't heard any complaints about this class since you started. I came up to see if you all were even in here."

I didn't have a pithy or even sarcastic response for either of them. The assistant principal was a Black man who seemed to really care about the students. He never demeaned them and seemed to really want to understand their perspectives when I heard him talking to students in the hallways. There was no magic spell—just an honest conversation, a group of students who had "had it," a teacher, some resources, and a classroom designed for them to assist each other, work as a community, and succeed.

7

Commentary on
Coach Cann's Narrative

In three consecutive Olympic games, 1992–2000, the U.S. men's basketball teams dominated international competition—winning the Olympic gold medal every four years. 1992 marked the first year that National Basketball Association (NBA) professional players could play in the Olympics; prior to 1992, basketball (like most other Olympic sports) limited participation to amateur athletes. As predicted, with this policy change, the U.S. men's teams ran away with the gold medals. Dubbed the "Dream Teams," the men's basketball teams brought together the best players in each position from the different NBA teams including Magic Johnson and Larry Bird (from the famed rival Lakers and Celtics teams, respectively), Patrick Ewing, Michael Jordan and Scottie Pippen, the Admiral (David Robinson), Clyde Drexler, Karl "the Mailman" Malone, John Stockton, Chris Mullen, Charles Barkley, and Christian Laettner.

In 2004, though, the dream turned into a nightmare with the U.S. men's basketball team losing enough preliminary games to fall out of con-

Reflections From the Field, pages 55–60

tention for the gold medal. Though several professional players declined to play in the 2004 games (most notably Kobe Bryant and Kevin Garnett), the team had retained many talented players such as all-stars Tim Duncan and Allen Iverson as well as rising stars LeBron James, Carmelo Anthony, Dwayne Wade, and Amar'e Stoudemire. Although young, the roster was formidable and they were favored (as in the previous three Olympic games) to win the gold. However, in their first game, the U.S. men's team was defeated soundly by Puerto Rico, 92–73. Despite this loss, they managed to play their way back into medal contention and were well on their way to the final game—that is, until they met Argentina in the quarterfinals. Other than NBA star Manu Ginobli, the level of talent on the Argentina team was no match for the NBA caliber that filled the roster of the U.S. men's team. The coach for the Argentina team, realizing this, prepared a game plan that incorporated powerful defense, consistent blocking out, and a tight screen-setting offense. And they won, 89–81, not because they were a talent powerhouse, but because they played as a team. Argentina showed that working as a team is more critical than a roster of superstars who play as talented individuals. Indeed, learning from that loss, subsequent U.S. men's basketball teams demanded that their star talent commit to playing together as a team for multiple years. The U.S. coaching team learned, as did Coach Cann, that a winning team is far more than the sum of its star players; it requires looking past the status of individual players to find ways for them to complement each other's strengths.

Some might argue that the 2004 team would have won if Kobe Bryant and Kevin Garnett had agreed to play that year; similarly, one might read Coach Cann's narrative and be left with the conclusion that her "nightmare" club team might have had a winning season if it had been stacked with six star players rather than just two. Yet the U.S. men's team's coaches as well as Coach Cann pointed to team dynamics rather than individual players as the key to a competitive team. Coach Cann contended in her narrative that her club team never played as a team. In fact, her junior varsity "dream" team, with inexperienced, mediocre, mid-sized players, was the team that almost went to finals. The difference? As a coach, she was forced (as was Argentina) to focus on the team dynamics rather than rely on individual talent to defeat rivals. With star players on the club team, she fell into the nightmare team trap and neglected to develop the entire team, much like the 2004 U.S. Olympic basketball team.

* * *

During the club season, Coach Cann worked with a heterogeneous group of volleyball players. What was predicted to be the dream team of the club fell apart, and the star players left the team prior to the end of the season. Status differences among the players worked against team goals much like status differences in heterogeneous classrooms can work against the achievement of academic goals if teachers do not attend to these differences with specific pedagogical practices. Drawing on the work of Berger, Cohen, and Zelditch, Jr. (1966, 1972), Cohen and Lotan (1995) described how status differences in heterogeneous classrooms led to problems among youth. Initial differences in talent, knowledge, or skills create an aura of high expectations for high performance, particularly on high-stakes tasks for which those talents are most relevant. These initial differences affect the participation of students differentially; high-status students participate more and, thus, learn more (Cohen, Lotan, & Leechor, 1989), while low-status students participate infrequently and, thus, learn less. Cohen and Lotan (1995) explained:

> Because of differences in perceived ability, the high-status student will then expect to be more competent and will be expected to be more competent by others. The next effect is a self-fulfilling prophecy whereby those who are seen as having *more ability relative to the group* in schoolwork or in reading tend to dominate those who are seen as having *less ability relative to the group* in schoolwork or reading. (p. 101, emphasis in original)

This is precisely what happened on Coach Cann's club team. The star players, assured in their star status, increased their participation, taking passes and hits that were not theirs. A response identity was created in the other players on the team whereby they began to defer to the other players' star status on the team. Coach Cann reinforced the status differences by strategizing around the two star players—even in their absences at practices—thus publicly affirming their star status.

During the club season, the status differences tore her team apart. As she wrote in her narrative, Coach Cann failed to build the necessary dependencies among her players; a critical membership was not created. Indeed, by building her team around the two star players—players who ultimately left the team—she exacerbated the status differences.

* * *

On her junior varsity team, there were surely some players who were more talented than others. There exists no true homogeneous grouping of athletes or students. Yet Coach Cann perceived that there were no star players who could carry the team. And so, like Argentina, she devised strategies that called on players to truly play as a team, fostering the *necessary dependencies* missing from her club team. As she wrote: "Each player on the court was integral at that moment in time for other players to be successful in getting the point or the side-out" (see Chapter 6). The creation of the necessary dependencies built a sense of team cohesion.

This cohesion is as important in the classroom as it is on the court. The pedagogy used with Coach Cann's junior varsity team mirrors the research on effective pedagogy in heterogeneous classrooms. Cohen and Lotan (1995) described a pedagogy they termed "complex instruction" used by elementary teachers in heterogeneous classrooms. Cohen, Lotan, Scarloss, and Arellano (1999) defined complex instruction as instruction that creates a classroom setting and interactions that encourage deeper comprehension, more equitable relationships among peers, and higher student achievement than that achieved in tracked classrooms. An alternative to tracking, complex instruction in heterogeneous classrooms allows all students to be academically challenged without exacerbating preexisting (or creating new) status differences among youth in the classroom.

In complex instruction, teachers design projects and tasks for groups that purposefully require the diverse abilities of all students in the group: "Multiple-ability tasks are a necessary condition for teachers to be able to convince their students that there are different ways to be 'smart'" (Cohen et al., 1999, p. 83). A pace and "'hustle and bustle' is created such that students must depend on one another to get the job done. . . . Students learn that they have the duty to assist those who ask for help" (p. 83). Interdependencies lead to no one working alone or slacking off; everyone becomes critical to the success of the entire group. They become, in essence, a team. Like the Argentina basketball team and Coach Cann's junior varsity team, students in the group know that the only way to complete the assigned task is to help each other achieve her or his best; no single student can lead them to a successful outcome.

Similarly, employing a rigorous curriculum that challenged all learners in her heterogeneous English classes, Joan Cone discussed how she scaffolded the learning of her students across status differences (Cone, 2006, p. 55). She focused as much on how to work together in the classroom space as she did on basic skill development and the development of analytical thinking, creating the opportunity for students to appreciate each other's contributions regardless of initial status differences.

In her 2006 study of mathematics departments that detracked their classes, Horn found that one department successful in raising student achievement worked together to find "group-worthy problems" that emphasized concepts and, similar to complex instruction, required creativity (rather than one learning modality) to solve. Thus, the student groups were forced to rely on all members of the group to get tasks completed as no one person in the group could solve the entire problem alone. Coach Cann's junior varsity team took the work of playing volleyball as "group-worthy work" which Horn defined as work that "draws effectively on the collective resources" of the group (Horn, 2006, p. 76).

Horn also found that mathematics departments successful in detracking their courses were careful to decouple mathematics knowledge from traditional notions of what it means to be a good student. Prior research on mathematics departments (Cann, 2012) confirms that mathematics teachers are partial to working with and thinking highly of students who know how to be a good student; that is, they know to write in pencil, put their names on their homework, and sit quietly at their desks. They do not expect to actively engage in their own learning. Departments successful at detracking their courses questioned those practices as necessary for success.

Maika Watanabe and colleagues (Watanabe, Nunes, Mebane, Scalise, & Claesgens, 2007), looking at the classroom teaching practices and beliefs of chemistry teachers in a school with a history of successful detracking, also found that teachers of successfully detracked classrooms think differently about what makes a student successful. Specifically, they found that these teachers hold a deep belief in the ability of their youth to learn; they do not hold static conceptions of knowledge, but rather believe in a "developmental...conception of ability and intelligence" (p. 693). Working with her junior varsity team, Coach Cann held tightly to the belief that her players could achieve if they worked hard and built their talents as a team. A strong player was redefined as one who asked for the ball, was willing to be aggressive, hustled 100% of the time, and was supportive of and encouraged her teammates.

*   *   *

On her junior varsity team, Coach Cann fostered a necessary trust among players on the court so that each person on the team valued and relied on the contributions of others regardless of their role. There was no such thing as the strongest player on the team, but the strongest player for that role in that play. Indeed, the concept of strength broadened. It was no longer just scoring, nor even simply athleticism that was recognized and valued for the team as a whole; rather, encouragement, questioning, and appreciation became strength attributes. During practices and study table, players were responsible for the well-being of other players, helping each other in drills, sharing skills, and completing homework together. Helping a player maintain academic eligibility was no less important than scoring points. Their success as a team was due to the sense of *critical membership* that was created among the team players. By critical membership, Coach Cann meant membership that was essential to the central task of the community. Each player felt and was critical to the success of the community.

From this experience with her junior varsity team, Coach Cann identified concrete strategies to use in her mathematics classroom years later. First, she redefined what it meant to be a good mathematics student as one who asked questions, pushed her to provide useful explanations, and helped others achieve their best. As well, she created the ultimate group-worthy task—to get the entire class to complete a year-long algebra course in under two months. Finally, she created a community of learners who relied on each other as much as her for support and guidance. She encouraged necessary dependencies among students and made it clear through her structures that each member of the class was critical to the success of others.

And, importantly, Coach Cann engaged in honest conversations about institutional racism. She did not underestimate the ability of her students to see and understand the "education debt" (Ladson-Billings, 2006) accrued to urban youth. She not only engaged in this important discussion with youth, but devised a plan for them to work together against the immediate resource debt forced upon them—they had had no regular, consistent mathematics teacher all year. She both acknowledged the structural challenge and modeled agency.

Above all, she revealed the important role of the teacher and coach in the classroom and on the court. While it is important to see our students as unique individuals, it is even more important to see the class as a team that will achieve the most success when they work and compete together in ways that build them up to more than a collection of individual talents.

8

Lessons From the Soccer Field

Eric J. DeMeulenaere
Clark University

In the mid-1980s as a college student, I saw Michael Jordan play in Chicago. I watched him slash to the hoop and fire up fade-away shots from the perimeter. In the first game I saw, he scored over fifty points in an amazing display of athleticism. But the Bulls still lost the game. In fact, even though Jordan was breaking scoring and defensive records, his team still had a losing record. Phil Jackson became the coach for the Bulls in the 1989–1990 season. After Phil Jackson arrived, Michael Jordan's individual stats, particularly scoring, declined, but the Bulls began to win. Under Jackson's coaching, Michael Jordan went from being an amazing individual player to a team leader. It was only when Jordan stepped into his role as the leader on the court that the Bulls became dominant champions.

It was not until my fifth year as a teacher that some of my students prevailed upon me to start a girls' soccer team. As a high school history teacher who saw over 150 students each day and as the coordinator of the school's student government, I was busy enough struggling to design lessons, grade a

Reflections From the Field, pages 61–68

never-ending stream of essays, and coordinate the student council. Besides, they were just a small group of girls, not even enough to make up a full soccer team. But they were persistent and skilled at constructing airtight arguments, as only teenagers are. They listed all the indisputable reasons why I needed to coach a new team. They argued that I needed the workout as much as they needed a coach; why pay money for a gym membership when I could run back and forth across the grass field? I wouldn't need to handle the logistics of running a team; they had recruited their mathematics teacher to attend to all of the league coaches' meetings and handle the bureaucratic headaches of managing a team. Breaking down the last of my hesitation, they argued, "It's a form of gender discrimination that the boys have a team and we don't!" That got to me and I agreed to "look into it."

The school's athletic director said that he would love to have a girls' soccer team, but he had no one to coach it. What could I say? I reluctantly told the girls that if they could recruit a full team, then I would coach it. Thus began my athletic coaching career, which taught me more about teaching than I ever expected. Among the many lessons that coaching taught me was that effective coaches develop the leadership and moral authority of their strongest players on and off the field. In this chapter, I explore these experiences from the field and then discuss how they played out in the classroom and school building.

The First Practice

> *I vividly remember the first day of tryouts for the varsity soccer team at my high school in Anchorage, Alaska. The first week, we didn't even touch a soccer ball. On day one in mid-March, the coach ran us through stretches and then gave us a map for a five-mile run. The cold Alaskan winter was slow to recede, so, as we ran, our warm breath clouded the frosty air. We jumped dirty snow banks at each street corner, caking my brand new Adidas turf shoes with mud. I was never one for long-distance running, but I knew that if I wanted to make the team, I needed to finish towards the front of the pack. So I ran hard. Five miles later, I walked in circles trying to make the pounding in my head return to my chest. I had finished this, our first challenge, near the front.*

Girls' soccer season in San Francisco likewise occurred in the spring. Monday afternoon in late February, an overcast day followed the rainy weekend, so the soccer field remained muddy. Even counting the girls who had yet to turn in their permission-to-participate forms, we still didn't have enough players to field a team. However, we were scheduled to start practice. And so, Monday afternoon, in the corner of my classroom away from the window, I exchanged my teacher uniform for sweats and cleats. I placed the ubiquitous marker of a coach, my lanyard with a whistle, around my neck and walked down to the field. The girls began to assemble, the rhythmic clunk of their backpacks hitting the aluminum bleachers mixing with Mexican Spanish stretching between girl players and boy spectators. Long dark hair was pulled back into ponytails with nervous energy. I, too, was anxious. I replayed in my head the speeches that my varsity soccer coach had given on our first day of practice. I had been a part of a competitive soccer program with a strong reputation that demanded hard work to even make the soccer team. I competed for a spot on the team with kids who, like me, had played soccer their entire childhoods. Now I was the coach of a fledgling soccer team that didn't yet have enough girls to form an organized team. Only two players had ever played on a competitive athletic team before. I looked at my watch. Three o'clock: start time. I looked up to where the girls were assembled. One girl was looking in her compact mirror adjusting her makeup. I shook my head and blew my whistle. "Jog around the field two times and then bring it in for stretching," I shouted. There was some good-natured grumbling from the girls and teasing from the boys. But every girl made her way down the bleachers, onto the field and started a slow jog around the field.

As they rounded the nearside of the field closest to the bleachers, the group of boys yelled, "¡Corran! C'mon, let's see you run!" The girls giggled and yelled back, but they didn't pick up their pace. Several girls started walking before they had finished the second lap. As I watched this all play out in the first ten minutes of our first practice together, I realized that the coach's speech that I had in mind wasn't going to work. As the players trickled in, I called them to the center of the field. They slowly assembled, breathing hard, hands on their sides. In the circle, bent over to catch their breath, they looked up at me, many with thick black mascara and eye-liner extended past the corner of their eyes. I wish I could say that I offered some memorized quote about heart or believing in themselves; but this wasn't a Hollywood movie and I was too overwhelmed with the amount of work we had yet to do to think of some inspirational speech. I had them form a circle and walked them through a series of stretches, having them count together with each stretch—we would become a team and create unity in all that we did. I then ran them through several drills. I had to teach them the basic rules and fundamentals of kicking, trapping, and dribbling a soccer ball.

At the end of the practice, I had them run sprints for conditioning. My screams and admonitions could not seem to get most of them to move faster than a jog. I ran after them, threatening to make them run more if I caught them, but that did not seem to motivate them as they just slowly jogged the extra sprints. I was seriously frightened for the first game that now seemed right upon us. Four weeks would not be enough time to get ready.

Building a Team

The next day I increased my recruiting pressure on three senior girls I had worked with since their freshman year in student government. They had never played soccer, but they were hard workers and two of them were good athletes. Weeks earlier, I had lightly suggested that they join the team. They had been on the fence about it; but after seeing our first practice, I knew I needed them off the fence and on our team.

By the end of the first week of practice, I had three new players and had kicked out the male spectators. However, we were still far from being a coherent team and all except the three seniors were still jogging their way through practice. I was distressed by the imminent clobbering that seemed to be fast approaching. The players only got excited in practice when talking about the different colors available for a new pair of cleats, whether we could all get practice shirts and in what color, and when we would get our uniforms. I was still struggling to get many of the players to understand how to make a throw-in and what "off-sides" meant. Despite my warnings and threats, they had no idea what was in store for them in our first game of the season.

There were, though, two signs of hope. The three seniors I brought on board really tried hard and, one of them, Marilyn, developed quickly. Her timing was good and she was not afraid to plow someone over to get the ball. I made her team captain, responsible for leading the stretches and serving as my coach on the field. Without my explicit direction, Marilyn began to encourage the other players to try harder through both her example and her words. In practice scrimmages, she would shout at her teammates to steal a ball, and her teammates responded.

By now I had figured out that part of my work was to toughen up these girls who had little collective experience in competitive sports. So instead of running simple sprints, I made them run and, on the whistle, dive to the ground, get back up and go the other direction repeatedly until they were exhausted and muddy. Marilyn ran her heart out in these conditioning exercises, and as she rose time and again from the mud, she rose to greater leadership. The other players watched her and began to emulate her intensity and drive. Not everyone was giving their all in practice, but I noticed that players were leaving the field dirty and sweaty and I was hearing fewer conversations about soccer attire and seeing fewer students check their makeup before practice.

Game Time

I was never a star on my varsity basketball team. No plays were run for me—I didn't have a great shot. I was never the big scorer. My points came from hustle. I played tough defense and I scrambled for rebounds. I worked hard for my few points and rebounds. I used to look with envy at Terry Caulkin, our leading scorer. He could run to the baseline and fire up shot after shot with a graceful pigeon-toed shooting stance. I used to wish that I could fire it up like Terry. That year, we made the play-offs, but lost in the second round in an excruciating double overtime.

My high school team, though, went on to win the state championship the year after I graduated. When I saw my coach the following summer, I joked, "Good thing you got rid of the dead weight like me so you could go on to win the championship." He didn't laugh, but instead looked me in the eyes and said seriously, "You weren't the reason we didn't win. Our problem last year was that we had players with too much ego. We won state because we didn't have any stars. We had to learn how to work hard and work together to win."

In a very short time, we came to our first game—an experience that served to educate our players perhaps more than my coaching had over the past month. The 13–0 clobbering and on-field exhaustion created a powerful learning moment. After the loss, in our team huddle, I struggled to give a speech that did not scream, "I told you so." So, I asked our team captain to say a few words. Marilyn stood there with strands of black hair sticking to her sweaty, flushed face, her clothes covered in mud and grass stains. Her teammates had just seen her leave her heart on the field. And the first words she spoke were an apology to the team.

"Sure, they were better than us, but I know I could have stopped at least two of their goals. I just messed up. I need to work harder as a full-back to never let a team score an easy goal. I need to step up in practice so I won't get so tired on the field." Her teammates jumped to her defense telling her she played really well. And she replied sternly with strong conviction, "I can do better. We all can do better."

There was silence. It was a tense moment that provided the turning point that we needed. Marilyn's words, combined with her example, were more powerful inspiration than any words I could offer. And her words taught me a lot about coaching.

The next practice students worked harder and got tougher. We were shut out our second game, but we played better and we were not dominated as we had been in the first game. In our third game we scored our first goal. Several weeks later we held our own against the only undefeated team in the league, losing, but not as badly as some of the other teams had. We even won a couple of games by the end of the season.

I learned a lot as a coach that season—lessons that I eventually translated into my classroom as a teacher and into my school when I became a principal. I had to contend with the challenges of my players' inexperience, poor training, extremely diverse skill levels, and a lack of adequate supplies. These challenges that confronted me on the field that first day were no different than the challenges that often confront urban teachers on the first day of school each year. Much like the other authors in this volume, I learned about being honest (see Chapter 4), about thinking and acting like a winner before you can be one (see Chapter 2), and about the need to recognize each player's individual strengths to coach her accordingly (see Chapter 6).

But perhaps the most profound lesson I learned from the field was that I had to build my team around the strongest players. To improve the team, I needed to cultivate both the soccer skills and the leadership of Marilyn if I wanted the rest of the team to elevate their game. I needed to cultivate the moral authority of my strongest player to make her the coach on the field. Unlike anything that I could say as a coach, the words of this player-leader were coupled with her actions, with herself as a role model. That is where her moral authority derived from. As a coach, I remained on the sidelines. A player-leader is in the same game, sweating, pushing, elbowing, struggling, and triumphing alongside her teammates. Her words carried a different weight.

From the Field to the Classroom

Building the leadership capacity of those on the field is no more important than in my classroom. Realizing that I did not have to be (nor should be) the only educator in my classroom was the beginning of my growth as a teacher. I took the lessons I learned on the field and brought them into the classroom when I was teaching later at a middle school in East Oakland.

This classroom had over thirty students, most of whom spoke Spanish as their first language, and all but one qualified for free and reduced price lunch. I was the newest teacher in the building, so in this classroom also sat a student named Edgar—"the most challenging student in the school," according to the principal. Edgar's former teachers were at a loss for how to support his learning. Labeled "defiant," rumor had it that Edgar was so defiant that he would sometimes not even go to the office when a teacher would send him out; the principal would have to come get him.

In the first weeks of school, I made it a point to get to know Edgar well and to make sure that I addressed his academic and social needs. I met with him individually and made my high expectations clear. I drove him home from school regularly—even though his apartment was nearby. I talked with his guardian. I individualized my assignments for him. Some of these efforts worked. But, at times, he would shut down and stop doing his work. At these times, he would distract other students.

It was not until I had students work on collaborative projects that I began to see true, consistent improvement in Edgar's behavior and academic performance. I strategically placed Edgar with another student, Carlos, who was two years older (Carlos had been held back in early elementary school). Carlos was physically the biggest student in the school. His size, athleticism, and mature presence earned him respect among the students; he was entrusted with the responsibility of coordinating the lunchtime sports activities. He was the student who would holler in a classroom for the other kids to "shut up," and all the students would listen.

Though the biggest and oldest, Carlos was not the highest-achieving academic student in the class. In a neighboring classroom, which was regularly out of control, Carlos was often the instigator of the disruptions. While I didn't have such challenges with Carlos in my classroom, I did regularly battle with him to get his homework in and put more effort into his assignments.

What ended up working best for both Carlos and Edgar was when I partnered the two together for a project. I went to Carlos with my concern of getting Edgar to produce high-quality work. Carlos was well aware of Edgar's behavior and performance in class and in the school. I enlisted Carlos' help to get Edgar to work with him on the project and to complete outstanding work. Carlos was more than willing to oblige.

When I called out their partner pair in class, Carlos pointed to a seat near him, and Edgar immediately joined him. And then they both focused together on the project—getting their work done. Never had either of them worked so diligently on an assignment. They not only sustained their focus for several days, but they produced thoughtful work.

Conclusion

Our success as a soccer team owed much to the leadership of Marilyn just as Edgar's academic success depended on Carlos. As an educator, it was when I put my ego aside and allowed my player-leaders and student-leaders to guide the way for other students that my teams and classrooms succeeded.

Any failure on my part to recognize, support, and develop the leadership of those I seek to educate is a failure on my part to be an effective coach, teacher, or school leader. Indeed, it was the ability to recognize and build on the existing leadership that made these experiences successful.

Coaching taught me a lot about teaching. Of course, I have had to learn this lesson over and over again as my ego has too often gotten in the way of what Marilyn taught me. Despite the Hollywood portrayal of successful coaches, my own effectiveness as a coach was not based on inspirational speeches or dynamism as a leader, but rather how I created space for my players to rise up as coaches on the field. As I reflect on my own trajectory as an educator over the past two decades, I realize that my effectiveness has been linked to the lessons that Marilyn offered in my first year as a soccer coach. Such reflections force humility, for I recognize that my successes are indebted to others and the failures occurred when I tried to lead alone.

9

Commentary on Coach DeMeulenaere's Narrative

Now this is the law of the jungle, as old and as true as the sky,
and the wolf that keeps it shall prosper and the wolf that doesn't shall die. . . .
The law runneth forward and back. For the strength of the pack is the wolf
and the strength of the wolf is the pack.

—Phil Jackson, quoting Rudyard Kipling (Olegario, 2007)

In 1914, *New Republic* author Randolph Bourne stepped into what, at the time, was the rather new social reality of the high school classroom and eloquently captured the essence of that environment. His classroom portrait depicted the timeless social norms of most high school classrooms across the U.S., and the present-day reader is left stunned to realize how little has changed in the intervening century to effect the social dynamics of the high school classroom. Of course the linkages to factories might seem outdated to our post-industrial stance, but the classroom structures have persevered despite larger economic transformations. He wrote:

Reflections From the Field, pages 69–75

> Here were these thirty children, all more or less acquainted.... Yet they were forced, in accordance with some principle of order, to sit at these stiff little desks, equidistantly apart, and prevented under penalty from communicating with each other. All the lines between them were supposed to be broken. Each existed for the teacher alone. In this incorrigibly social atmosphere, with all the personal influences playing around, they were supposed to be, not a network or a group, but a collection of things, in relation only with the teacher. (Bourne, 1914, p. 24)

His 1914 portrayal is relevant to the social and environmental reality of most classrooms today, typically designed to limit student interaction. Indeed, the only interaction that is valued in the classroom is that between the teacher and student. While the teacher–student relationship is incredibly important, as evidenced by the other narratives in this volume, it is not the only significant relationship in the classroom (or on the athletic field).

Coach DeMeulenaere's narrative focused on the need for coaches (and teachers) to encourage interaction among teammates on sports teams (and among students in classrooms). His narrative recognized that peer leadership plays a valuable role in inspiring other players to take risks on the field. As a coach, his own efforts to model intensity were only minimally effective in motivating his players to increase their own intensity. He was in that instance, perhaps, too distant from his players' lived realities for them to see him as an authentic role model on the soccer field. Neither was he in the game with them, struggling and facing the same frustrations. Thus, his story was about a coach who came to realize that he was most effective for his players when he embraced his position on the sidelines. He was most influential in his work developing peer leaders or, rather, "coaches on the field."

The "Classroom Management" Framework

Struggling teachers, novice and veteran alike, often identify "classroom management" as their greatest challenge (Bushaw & McNee, 2009; Marzano, Marzano, & Pickering, 2003). They argue that students, particularly those in high school, socialize with each other in ways unrelated to their assigned learning task. Hence, at fault are the frequent (and, as they see it, inappropriate) student-to-student interactions.

In *Discipline and Punish*, Foucault (1995) examined micro-level interactions in societal institutions such as schools to explore the myriad ways that power is displayed in modern societies. His analyses revealed that schools are remarkably similar to hospitals, factories, asylums, military barracks, and prisons. Indeed, the disciplinary regime manifest in these institutions attempt to create docile, *controllable* bodies through strict attention to how these institutions distribute individuals throughout spaces and define the activities of these individuals.

The architectural metaphor for this control is seen in the plans for Jeremy Bentham's *panopticon* prison, in which prison cells were sketched encircling a guard tower. From the vantage point of the tower, guards would be able to observe the cells and their inhabitants; however, the imprisoned individuals would be unable to see the guard and unable to tell when the guard actually observed their cells. The inmates were thus placed in the position of monitoring their own behavior, ever worried that at any moment the guard might observe their actions. In this way, one individual guard could manage a large number of imprisoned individuals.

To capture the classroom version of this disciplinary apparatus, Foucault offered an illustration of the auditorium in the Fresnes prison. In the image, an educator lectures to students about the evils of alcoholism from the front of a lecture hall with a security guard stationed to his right. The audience is filled with students arranged in terraced seating except there are no chairs; instead, the students are placed in rising rows of individual wooden boxes with small openings through which they see only the instructor. Students are physically forced, in Bourne's words, to be "in relation only with the teacher" (1914, p. 24).

While such an illustration captures Foucault's penchant for extremes, it is also more similar than not to the high school classrooms described by Bourne (and all too similar to modern day high school classrooms). Classrooms in most high schools are arranged off long hallways with a single window in the door through which administrators can observe both students and teachers. Within these rooms, desks are typically arranged in rows facing the front of the classroom. Students are discouraged, by the physical arrangement, from socializing with students in front of and behind them. As well, from their location at the front of the room, teachers can monitor interactions among students. Further, the rules and norms of such classrooms discourage dialogue among students while encouraging dialogue between teacher and students. The rhythm of this dialogue often takes the form of the teacher asking a question, students raising hands to indicate their desire to respond, the teacher selecting and calling on one student, and the student responding. The teacher, alone, decides whether the submitted response is correct (see Cazden, 2001 for more on this classroom discourse pattern).

This model of the classroom allows a single teacher to monitor, examine, and control large groups of children; the bells, the egg-carton classrooms off long corridors, the rows of desks, and the hand-raising create an efficient, factory-like production model of education. Indeed, with the current underfunding of public schools, it is not uncommon to find classrooms with over forty students with one teacher (Dillon, 2011; Owen, 2011).

Students learn to adapt to the educational panopticon early on. A few years ago, Herbert Kohl (2009) visited an urban school where elementary-aged Black and Brown youth were required to line up for lunch with their arms crossed over their chests such that their hands held their shoulders. His colleague noted that she had seen imprisoned men line up the same way on her recent visit to a prison. When Kohl asked a teacher about this practice, the teacher confirmed that the school had borrowed the idea from prison practices. While such policies are extreme, they call attention to Foucault's insights into the surveillance and control mechanisms in schools today, which, though perhaps more subtle, are further maintained by high-stakes testing, scripted curricula, and the monitoring of teacher performance (Kohn, 2012). Add to this zero-tolerance policies for behavior, and we see how the educational panopticon manifests in schools and how insightful Foucault's associations between schools and prisons, military barracks, and factories were.

The educational panopticon works to separate and monitor students to better create *individuals* who can be observed, controlled, and evaluated. Foucault's framing captured the ways that educational controls function to oppress students (and teachers). However, if we were to read only Foucault, we would fail to see that indeed, as Bourne so clearly recognized later in his work, students have agency. They do not sit compliant to the forces of control. Students resist the systems of control and assert their humanity by defying the educational panopticon.

The Classroom Community Framework

In contrast to the disciplinary methods enacted on youth in schools, methods to build community among youth have been proposed by researchers. In this framework, a classroom is conceived of as a community of practice, and individuals in such communities "define with each other what constitutes competence in a given context" (Wenger, 2003, p. 80). This definition of competence is negotiated by members of the community and, despite what a teacher might attempt to externally impose, expresses how the community itself views competence. Though newcomers to these established communities are often influenced by community norms determined prior to their arrival, even newcomers, in subtle ways, are able to shape the community. Learning within a community of practice is, therefore, *situated learning* (Lave & Wenger, 1991)—learning that is specific to that particular context and community. Learning is defined by the expectations of the members of the community and the meaning negotiated constantly.

This idea of a community of practice is exhibited in Coach DeMeulenaere's portrayal of his soccer team in unexpected ways. Most of his players had limited experience playing soccer, being members of a team, and playing competitive sports generally. Thus, they were unfamiliar with this type of community of practice. They brought with them, to the first days of practice, other ways of being that were relevant to other contexts—for instance, the classroom. Their new understandings of competence evolved from previous experiences in different contexts, what they learned from their coach (a peripheral member of their community), and each other. However, when a more experienced athlete joined the team and brought with her notions of competence informed by other sporting communities of practice, the members of the soccer team were apprenticed into the work of being an athlete, and a new definition of competence emerged. This experienced athlete was seen as a legitimate participant in the community, one whose efforts and hard work were worth emulating.

Early in the soccer season, Coach DeMeulenaere recognized that his team of novice athletes lacked players who were experienced, longtime members of a sporting community of practice. There were no players who could lead the way for the team and inspire novice players to grow in meaningful ways. He attempted, initially, to fill that role himself and to initiate the team into the athletic community of practice. However, as the coach on the periphery, he was not viewed as a legitimate participant of their community. He was perhaps a teacher and a guide, but he was not a member of the community in the same way as the players.

He recognized this and recruited older athletes from other sports to the soccer team. And it was Marilyn, a dedicated athlete, who brought new notions of competency to their team and emerged as a leader. At the end of the first game, when the players experienced their first defeat, it was her speech that shifted the understanding of competency. Her dissatisfaction with her own efforts shifted the community of practice, causing the other players to change how they viewed their efforts, even their identity as soccer players.

Coach DeMeulenaere's successful development of the team resulted from his understanding and ability to build a stronger community of practice by inviting experienced players to the team. Such work could only be done, though, with a clear understanding of the dynamics among the members of the community. It is critical to identify, legitimize, and exalt the right players and to develop them as leaders and not just players. As well, it is important to attend to how and why one singles out leaders such that doing so does not undermine the team as a whole. For example, Phil Jackson, quoted at the beginning of this chapter, is recognized as one of the greatest coaches of any sport not only for his eleven professional championships, but because he made highly talented teams become championship teams. Jackson joined the Bulls after Michael Jordon was an established star player but before the Bulls had achieved success. He joined the Lakers after Shaq and Kobe had played three seasons together. His greatness was not from building a talented roster; it was from taking a talented roster and making it a championship team. He achieved this by making his talented players into leaders. Jackson was famous for walking away from a time-out and letting his player-leaders talk with the team. He was known for emphasizing not the great shot or even the assist, but the pass that set up the assist and shot. He did not exalt Jordon, Pippen, Kobe, or O'Neil for their athletic performance; that was already established. He exalted them for their leadership. He made them the coaches on the court—experienced members of their community of practice.

Jackson knew his work was to get the team playing together. He did that through quiet conversations with his leaders between games and practice sessions. In the words of Kobe Bryant, Phil Jackson was "absolutely brilliant at bringing a group together to accomplish one common goal" (quoted in Williams, 2011).

New Models of Leadership

Just as the media is replete with images of inspirational coaches, so too are there a plethora of similar images of teachers and school leaders who present strong charismatic models of leadership. This model of the strong and powerful leader inspiring students to reach unimaginable heights is proffered in education today. In Coach DeMeulenaere's narrative, we saw him begin his coaching experience striving to be just such a leader—passionately pushing his players to excel.

However, when that didn't provide the desired results, he stepped back to make room for and mentor Marilyn in a leadership role on their team. This reflected a different style of leadership than showcased in Hollywood movies and in many classrooms and on many soccer fields. It is about coaches and teachers decentering themselves and fostering the leadership of youth. Coach DeMeulenaere recruited a player who could be a strong leader on the field. He also gave this leader the authority to take the lead. Recruiting Marilyn, making her team captain, and giving her time to speak after the first game were some of Coach DeMeulenaere's inspiring moves.

First and foremost, Coach DeMeulenaere's story revealed the important role of coaches and teachers to be keen sociological observers of their students. As John Dewey realized over a century ago, the "educational process has two sides—one psychological and one sociological; and...neither can be subordinated to the other or neglected without evil results following" (Dewey, 1897, p. 77). Effective coaches, effective pedagogues in all domains, must be social scientists of their classroom spaces. They need to understand the social dynamics that enable them to develop student leadership and foster strong classroom or team cultures. In Coach DeMeulenaere's narrative, he supported an experienced athlete who was driven and mature. Maintaining and understanding how to work the larger social dynamics becomes a critical and understudied aspect of effective coaching and teaching.

Part of this awareness of the social dynamics is understanding the potential for untapped leadership on the field and in the classroom and developing the classroom culture around it. In Gloria Ladson-Billings' (1994) analysis of culturally relevant teachers, she explored the way one teacher, Ms. Lewis, developed children labeled as "at-risk" into classroom leaders and stars. One example was the work she did with a student named Larry. He was the oldest child in the class because he had been held back several times. Other teachers had "referred to him as 'an accident waiting to happen' and none wanted him enrolled in their classrooms" (p. 111). Ms. Lewis called him a "piece of crystal," stating that the school had "been placing him in the kitchen junk drawer" but she wanted him "to be up there in the china cabinet" for everyone to see (p. 111). Ms. Lewis recognized his maturity and saw his potential. She elevated him to a leadership position in the classroom and he rose to it. By the end of the school year, he was earning all A's and B's, solving problems through peer conflict mediation, and elected as president of the sixth grade. Ms. Lewis recognized the social dynamics of the classroom, recognized Larry's potential for leadership, and cultivated it to the benefit of the classroom culture. Similarly, Coach DeMeulenaere recognized and cultivated the leadership in Marilyn and Carlos, resulting in a stronger culture for the team and classroom.

10

Reconciliations

In our first read of the coaching narratives presented in this book, we became worried. The stories seemed to contradict each other. We had four stories about effective practice on the field and in the classroom that seemed to have conflicting messages. Coach McDermott told us that winning has little to do with the score, while Coach Malone argued that the score is the most honest teacher. So which is it? Does the score matter or not? Coach Cann encountered problems on the volleyball court when she built her team around her strongest players, while Coach DeMeulenaere's team only found success when he developed leaders on the field. The narratives of Coaches McDermott, Malone and Cann revealed them to be charismatic leaders of their teams, while Coach DeMeulenaere was most effective as a coach when he stepped into the shadows allowing his player-leaders to step forward as motivating forces. So what, from these stories, are the collective takeaways? Can we learn anything from this collection of narratives that is more meaningful than a trope like, "Winning comes in different forms"?

Reflections From the Field, pages 77–83
Copyright © 2013 by Information Age Publishing

We think so. Indeed, when we dig deeper we find that the apparent contradictions exist only at the surface. In this chapter, we examine these differences and find that the narratives, at their core, reflected similar truths about effective coaching and teaching.

Does the Score Matter?

Coach McDermott titles his narrative, "Winning Has Little to Do with the Score." In his chapter, he argued that the score itself is not important. In fact, the score is irrelevant to the declaration of a winner; being a winner, instead, is determined by one's values, work ethic and integrity. By contrast, Coach Malone opened his narrative with the 90–6 defeat of the Lady Cougars basketball team; the score of this game told both the players and their new coach the truth about the amount of work they needed to do to become a winning team. In fact, the score mattered greatly because scoreboards often highlight painful truths no one is willing to speak. Patronizing students with small nods of sympathy lacked an imagination of what the players were capable of achieving.

Some might read Coach Malone's tale as confirmation that we need more test data, more scores, to measure where we are. Doing so, though, misses the point. The players and students know too well the score without glancing at the scoreboard. Where the standardized test movement and Coach Malone differ is in their understanding of what is useful about the score and, more importantly, what to do with the data. For Coach Malone, the score kept him honest and forced him to dig in to teach the foundational skills necessary to raise his students' writing to his college-ready expectations. We don't need scoreboards or standardized tests to tell us how we're doing in our urban schools. We simply need to acknowledge where we are and begin the hard work of increasing learning. Coach Malone does not need to the Massachusetts Comprehensive Assessment System test to tell him that the school system had failed to teach his students how to write. What we lack is not evidence, but the courage to face this reality. Our fear of facing this bleak reality derives from our uncertainty of just how to take our students from a 90–6 loss to a winning streak. This is indeed an awesome challenge when we know that schools have not been designed to support the academic success of Black and Brown, low-income, and/or immigrant youth. What Coach Malone shared in his narrative was his journey of *courage, creativity,* and *commitment* to a group of youth who have embraced the "loser" identity foisted upon them.

Coach McDermott, too, knew the score. The baseball team had lost every game during the previous season. The majority of his high school students came into his English class preliterate. He argued, in his narrative, that this score matters only to tell us what work needs to be done. He urged us to not invest in the score or the resulting "worst piece of shit" labels ascribed to our youth. Rather, by example, he encouraged us to show the *courage, creativity* and *commitment* necessary to develop long-term plans to transform the bleak into the hopeful.

This type of coaching is not efficient. It is not scripted, standardized, nor is it for everyone. It takes time, attention, passion, and love for the sport and for the youth with whom they work. It takes *courage* to acknowledge the institutional truths that affect urban youth—youth disproportionately affected by the historically collaborative efforts of racism and poverty. It takes imagination to envision alternative outcomes and the *creativity* to work around a system determined to undermine urban youth. And it takes the *commitment* to stay in the game despite a culture and bureaucracy that denigrates such courage, creativity, effort, and moral conviction.

Stars in Our Midst

After developing a successful junior varsity volleyball program, Coach Cann took charge of the top team in a club volleyball program. This team, itself touted as the star team of the program, included two star players who were exempted from the tryout process; thus, their star status was confirmed and firmly entrenched even before the club season began. And, despite missing many practices once the season was underway, club policy dictated that they be allowed to start and play in every game if their skills warranted it. Coach Cann, too, became invested in their star status and what their talents could potentially do for their season record. She built her team around these two players, using cones in place of the often-absent stars during practices. Their teammates, following the lead of their coach, also became invested in the stars' talents and, conversely, their own inability to measure up. And it was precisely the team's deference to these stars on the court that caused the chaos and defeat in game after game. Indeed, it was only after the two stars grew tired of losing and left the team that the others began to improve as individual players and as a team.

In contrast, Coach DeMeulenaere's team began with no stars. In fact, they began with virtually no athletes. Despite his efforts to teach them the rules of the game, build foundational skills, and increase stamina and strength, he could not instill a fierce desire to win. As a coach on the sidelines, he had little influence over their hearts. After a particularly painful loss, an experienced athlete on the team found a way into their hearts. Her own passion for the game and disappointment in her inability to make crucial plays motivated other players to work harder and play with heart. In the case of Coach DeMeulenaere's soccer team, it seemed that one star player, admired by her teammates, could lead a team to victories.

The narratives again seem to be in conflict. Does the presence of strong players hurt or help the development of a team? The answer to that question lies in the common underlying story of both narratives—a story about the organizational culture of these two teams. Coach Cann's and Coach DeMeulenaere's narratives revealed the critical role of the coach to attend to the social dynamics of the team and to use that knowledge to build cohesion. Their narratives also illustrated the power of strong players to undermine or build that cohesion. Most important, these two stories taught us that effective coaching, or teaching, is not only about being a social scientist on the field and in the classroom; it is also about the reinvention of the concept of leadership.

At the intersection of these two stories is a rearticulation of leadership. In Carter G. Woodson's conception, true leaders are actually the servants of those they lead:

> The servant of the people, unlike the leader, is not on a high horse elevated above the people and trying to carry them to some designated point to which he would like to go for his own advantage. The servant of the people is down among them, living as they live, doing what they do and enjoying what they enjoy. He may be a little better informed than some other members of the group; it may be that he has had some experience that they have not had, but in spite of this advantage he should have more humility than those whom he serves. (Woodson, 1933, p. 131)

This quote captures the difference between the stars on Coach Cann's club volleyball team and the player on Coach DeMeulenaere's soccer team who rose to a leadership position on the team. The stars on Coach Cann's club volleyball team refused to work "down among" the other players. In fact, they rarely even attended the practices. They showed up for games, took over, and carried the team to certain defeat. They were more skilled and experienced on the volleyball court, but they lacked the humility to truly serve the team. Instead, these stars saw themselves as the leaders and centers of the team, but being the stars of a losing team proved not worth their while.

Marilyn, the emerging leader on Coach DeMeulenaere's team, exemplified the type of leader that Woodson described as a servant. After playing her heart out only to witness their first loss, she humbly apologized for her mistakes and promised the team (and herself) to work harder during practices. She adopted the model of a leader who was the servant, humbly expecting and demanding more of herself. She didn't try to cajole her teammates to improve their playing; rather, she focused on how she could improve herself for the benefit of her team. And it is this humility coupled with her effort and strength that made her a true leader and inspired her teammates.

This perspective of leaders as servants plays out not only for the star players on the team; it holds true for the adults. Coaches and teachers, too, excel when they are invested in their players' growth and learning more so than their own image and win–loss record. This was reflected in all four narratives in this book. Coach Cann didn't begin to see growth in the players on her club team until she was forced to see that building her team around her star players created a response identity in her other players as "non-stars." She became convinced that the only way to win was to increase the playing time of their star players. Only when she focused on all of her players, after the stars left, did the program improve. Coach Malone put aside his Teacher of the Year jacket and parking space to roll up his sleeves and do the work necessary to teach his students to write. Coach McDermott sacrificed their shut-out game to teach his players to honor and respect the norms they had established on their team. He also put respect for his players above respect for rules that didn't make sense (rules that even jeopardized the safety of his players). Coach DeMeulenaere only found success as a coach when he stayed on the sidelines, allowing Marilyn to coach on the field. The first move of the servant coach is to listen, understand, and empathize with players.

Service is imbued with not only humility, but sacrifice as well. Marilyn's legitimacy as a leader emanated from her visible sacrifices on the field. Coach McDermott sacrificed his paycheck to purchase enough baseballs to allow his players to stay out of the field beyond the ballpark. It was through humble service and sacrifice that they became legitimate and trusted leaders. And only then did the players and students follow.

The Dynamic Coach at the Center of the Team?

In the stories told in this volume, we got glimpses of truly charismatic and dynamic coaching and teaching. In the dugout, for example, we witnessed Coach McDermott pulling Ares from pitching a perfect game because he broke a team norm. We heard Coach Malone's speeches when he took over the Lady Cougar's basketball team. We saw Coach Cann hitting volleyballs at her players, demanding that they "get down" and "get ready." These images conjure up many of the Hollywood images of strong, dynamic coaches at the center of their teams' programs.

These images contrast decidedly with Coach DeMeulenaere, who began his season struggling to be that strong and inspirational coach. He yelled and ran alongside his players to encourage them to run faster and work harder, but it didn't work. It was only when he stepped away from center stage and allowed one of his players to lead that his team was compelled to work harder. As well, Coaches Cann, McDermott, and Malone reflected the "teacher-at-the-center" philosophy that contradicts the "guide on the side," student-centered teaching advocated in much of the education literature (Zemelman, Daniels, & Hyde, 2012). Are their narratives a counterargument to constructivist teaching?

This contrast is at the heart of why we've written this book. We have sought to reclaim the metaphor of athletic coaching for teaching as it was originally offered by Ted Sizer three decades ago. Sizer (1984) wrote, "Ironically, it is the athletic coach, often arrogantly dismissed by some academic instructors as a kind of dumb ox, unworthy of being called a real teacher, who may be a school's most effective teacher" (p. 106). Since then, the metaphor has rarely been used in education to understand teaching. Rather, it has been associated with the role of school or literacy coaches to support teachers in more effective teaching. Often, in this context, coaches are brought in from the outside to help coach a teacher or school to success. In the wake of No Child Left Behind, numerous urban districts employ school coaches to help turn around the practices of teachers with low student test scores. Coaches are not demanding or authoritative; rather, they are framed as supportive and suggestive (Murphy & Datnow, 2003; Neufeld & Roper, 2003).

But this image of the coach in education is a far cry from most athletes' experiences with their own coaches. Athletic coaches are often not afraid to assert their authority, make speeches, engage in direct instruction, and take center stage. So what are we to make of this seeming contradiction? We argue that the coaching metaphor in education must embrace both the teacher-centered and student-centered; it is a false dichotomy that does not serve students (or players). The coaching metaphor reminds us that the players go out onto the field without their coaches. What the players know and are able to do are all that matter once on the field. Yet, how coaches prepare the players for performance is a complex process. Sometimes the coaches stand at the chalkboard and explain the plays while players listen. Sometimes the skills are demonstrated and modeled by the coaches. Sometimes players are asked to drill a skill over and over. And sometimes they scrimmage—they simulate the performance as it will be in the game. Coaches teach basketball plays on chalkboards and demonstrate where players should go, how to set the screen, and where to roll after the pick.

They might even walk through a play several times without any defense. But always, they want to see it enacted in a realistic environment. They bring in the B-team to play defense and see how the play works, how to correct mistakes, how to address contingencies. But it is all focused on making sure that the players know how to perform come game time.

In the classroom, this means that sometimes teachers will be front and center explaining how to do something. They may stay there to model it, but they must always have the students do it themselves. And then they must be beside students helping to correct mistakes and to improve so that students can perform on their own eventually. The coaching metaphor means that the focus is on getting students to the point where they can independently do the work. To do this, teachers need to take center stage at times.

11

Reflections From the Field and Classroom

In the commentary chapters for each narrative, we highlighted important educational ideas apparent in the corresponding narrative. In Chapter 3, we examined Coach McDermott's pedagogy of trust. We looked at the need for greater honesty over and above the call for more data in Chapter 5; we emphasized the need to accompany that honesty with a systematic approach focused narrowly on teaching students to do a few things extremely well. In our discussion of Coach Cann's narrative, we examined the social and emotional aspects of detracking classrooms and teaching in heterogeneous spaces. In Chapter 9, we explored the role of effective educators in developing the leadership of students.

In Chapter 10, we reconciled the seeming disjunctures in the lessons learned from the four coaching narratives in this book. In this present chapter, we conclude with a discussion of two final themes that bubbled to the surface in the four narratives as well as in the educational literature: the role of *authentic caring* and the responsibility of educators (and

Reflections From the Field, pages 85–93
Copyright © 2013 by Information Age Publishing
All rights of reproduction in any form reserved.

coaches) to engage in *praxis*, an ongoing cycle of reflection and action to-wards improved practice. These themes reflect the thinking and practices of effective educators. We explore each of these in turn and then consider their implications for a classroom pedagogy potentially powerful enough to disrupt the production of inequity in schools and, more specifically, in our urban schools.

Caring

Educational research on the pedagogy of teachers working with urban, Black and Brown, low-income, and/or immigrant youth suggests that a "pedagogy of poverty" (Haberman, 1991, 2010) is far too common. This pedagogy, reminiscent of Freire's banking pedagogy of the oppressed (1970), contributes to the reproduction of educational inequities.

Haberman argued that while there exists a variety of teaching methods used in urban classrooms ranging from the didactic to computer-assisted in-struction, there is a commonality in "basic urban style" defined by "a body of specific teacher acts" (p. 291). This pedagogy confines teacher actions to administrating and controlling time, space, student behavior, and student bodies through banking and instituting dehumanizing relationships with students (Foucault, 1995; Freire, 1970; Noddings, 2008).

Valenzuela (1999) argued that a pedagogy of poverty follows the struc-tural logic of a schooling system designed with "an attention to things and ideas" and an over-concern with the impersonal, noninclusive, and culturally irrelevant—what she refers to as "aesthetic caring" (p. 22). From her ethno-graphic work at Seguin High School, Valenzuela found that the Latino youth in her study, instead, longed to be cared for and to have teachers listen in-tently to their needs and respond with relevant and appropriate material. In short, they desired and responded to *authentic caring*, or *educación*.

Authentic caring derives from the work of theorists such as Nel Nod-dings (2008); it is a pedagogy that flows from the interests of students. Nod-dings (2008) argued that caring theory is concerned with the relationship between the cared for and the carer. It is marked by listening guided by the heart; the concerns of the cared for guide the work of the carer. Valenzuela (2005) wrote that with authentic caring, "learning is premised on a hu-mane and compassionate pedagogy inscribed in reciprocal relationships" (p. 92). Teachers build reciprocal and personal relationships with their stu-dents and are committed to their students' development as whole beings.

Antrop-González and De Jesús (2006) built on this notion of authentic caring, distinguishing between two types of caring that school communities in their study exhibited in their work with urban youth. The first, *soft caring*, described the attitude of school communities that ignore the very real power dynamics present in schools and society that result from poverty and racism. Ignoring the structural violence of poverty and racism, these schools are left without a political framework to understand the systemic problems that confront their students; so, instead, they pity their students and lower their expectations of what their students can achieve (Antrop-González & De Jesús, 2006). By contrast, educational communities that are successful with urban youth embrace a *critical care* and create "culturally additive learning communities underscored by high-quality relationships and high academic expectations that reflect an ethic of *critical* care and illustrate the practice of *hard* caring—a form of caring characterized by supportive instrumental relationships and high academic expectations" (Antrop-González & De Jesús, 2006, p. 413, emphasis in original).

In the four narratives in this volume, we found examples of this authentic, critical, hard caring, which we succinctly define as caring that is concerned with *meaningful, reciprocal relationships*; an acknowledgment of, discussion about, and *action against racism and classism* in the schooling institution; and the implementation of *high expectations and support structures* to ensure the high achievement of students.

Meaningful, Reciprocal Relationships Marked by Listening

In Chapter 4, we observed Coach Malone creating such relationships with both his basketball players and students. He not only acknowledged how the coaching staff and school failed the players (even though he had been named Teacher of the Year), but then he committed the time and resources to provide structure and support for improved performance on the court and in the classroom. Coach DeMeulenaere similarly created caring relationships with his soccer players and students. He listened carefully and then honored the requests of his female students to create a girls' soccer team, recruiting players and committing the time to build a program. He also recognized that his own voice as coach was not as powerful as the voice of his player-leader, who was able to motivate and push his team to greatness in ways that he could not. Listening intently to their needs, he nurtured this player-leadership rather than remain "center stage."

Acknowledging, Discussing, and Acting Against Institutional Oppression

From her ethnographic work at Seguin High School, Valenzuela added to this understanding of authentic caring a political dimension. She wrote:

> Students' cultural world and their structural position must also be fully ap-
> prehended, with school-based adults deliberately bringing issues of race,
> difference, and power into central focus. . . . A more profound and involved
> understanding of the socioeconomic, linguistic, sociocultural, and structur-
> al barriers that obstruct the mobility of Mexican youth needs to inform all
> caring relationships. (1999, p. 109)

Coach McDermott most clearly captured the political teacher identity as he repeatedly stood against an uncaring and bureaucratic school system that attempted to send his players into littered fields and promoted students from grade to grade without teaching them to read. He, like Valenzuela's students, understood the difference between schooling and *educación*; time and again, he sided with *educación*, often visibly challenging the racism and classism on the field and inside school walls.

With her students, Coach Cann took on the challenging conversation with students to make sense of the institutional racism of which they were all aware, but which had not been publicly acknowledged and discussed with students. She took it beyond the discussion when, like Coach McDer-mott, she provided the curriculum, resources, instruction, and support to make up for the learning lost over a year of substitute teachers.

High Expectations and Support Structures

Hard caring is seen throughout the narratives as well. It is reflected in Coach Malone's honest conversations with his players and students. He came to understand that while honesty was painful, dishonesty was cruel, because it didn't protect students; rather, it prevented them from directly engaging in the hard work to overcome challenges. When Coach Malone talked to his basketball players, he did not mince words on the poor perfor-mance he witnessed. But he also stepped in with a plan and commitment to turn things around.

Coach McDermott built a culture where students learned that they must complete thoughtful and difficult work. The standards were not lowered. Supports were provided, but the expectations remained high. And the con-sequences for not meeting them were severe; Ares was flunked for not turning in his work. It was clear to Ares that Coach McDermott cared for his students and baseball players, but Coach McDermott was anything but soft.

The substitute teachers who had taught prior to Coach Cann's arrival practiced soft care, if there was any care at all. They did not demand or inspire excellence. By contrast, Coach Cann expected her students to learn a year's worth of mathematics in two months, and she expected them to treat each other with respect and provide help to each other. And the students rose to those expectations. Hard care refuses to enable mediocrity; instead it believes in the highest potential of students and players and demands excellence and hard work until the students and players learn to believe in their own greatness. This hard care turned a losing baseball team into district and state champions. Coach Malone's basketball team went from a humiliating defeat to district playoffs in two years.

The success these coaches achieved in the gym and on the field and as teachers in the classroom was grounded in the authentic, critical, hard care articulated by Valenzuela, Noddings, and Antrop-González and De Jesús. Such a care decries and fights against the oppressive conditions that youth face; it also forces youth to work hard to overcome adversity. The work of the coaches and teachers featured herein embraced this authentic, critical, hard caring and, without it, they could never have achieved what they did with their students and players.

Teaching as Praxis

Paulo Freire (1970) defined praxis as "reflection and action upon the world in order to transform it" (p. 36). Without critical reflection guiding the actions, the work becomes "mere activism" (p. 52). The dialectic between critical reflection and action is necessary so that the work is authentic to the social and historical context. This is difficult and ongoing work, as Freire described: "Knowledge emerges only through invention and re-invention, through the restless, impatient, continuing, hopeful inquiry men [sic] pursue in the world, with the world, and with each other" (p. 58).

While Freire emphasized the emptiness of critical consciousness apart from action, here we focus on the importance of critical reflection in the work of teachers striving to be agents of transformation because teaching involves ongoing action in the world. The challenge for teachers is not to act, but to strive to ground those actions in critical reflection of the social and cultural realities they encounter in schools. The challenge is to make the action of teaching transformative rather than a disconnected activism. Thus, the call for praxis in teaching is a call for teachers to ground their practice in reflection. This requires that teachers and coaches become *so-*

cial scientists in their spaces, critically reading their environment and the social dynamics in their context. It also means that teachers must embrace a *Socratic disposition* such that they strive towards mastery.

Teacher/Coach as a Social Scientist

Effective coaches and teachers must understand the social dynamics at play within their context. The coaches/teachers in this volume revealed their keen ability to read and analyze their contexts and the accompanying dynamics. In Coach McDermott's very first practice, as Teddy ran laps with puffs of smoke trailing, Coach McDermott realized that the time he "had spent working on plays and batting and fielding and running and sliding and such" would not be his first priority (see Chapter 2). He recognized that he would have to find creative ways to address these social dynamics before he could move into the technical instruction.

Coach Malone's narrative was about learning how to honestly recognize the social reality of his team and in his classroom and then respond appropriately. He set up his winning team with more challenging rivals mid-season. He watched carefully as his team's composure evaporated after confronting a powerful and talented team. After the game, he let the players wrestle with their thoughts without making any comments. However, at the next practice, he began the process of analyzing what happened and rebuilding their confidence; he reminded them that they had the skills to represent themselves well against powerful opponents. When they went to district playoffs and again met a stronger team, they kept their composure and gave that team a run.

Reading her class was critical for Coach Cann's mathematics class. The students had been through several teachers and were still not prepared for high school mathematics. She had to think deeply about the classroom culture and design her action based on her critical read of the realities of institutional racism and tracking. Similarly, Coach DeMeulenaere learned from his own trial and error that he couldn't simply stipulate greater effort from his soccer players. He needed to understand the way that the community of practice defined competency and make space for legitimate participants to shift this understanding.

All of these coaches and teachers worked hard to understand the social context and developed their practice from that understanding. Their effectiveness resulted from reading their communities and social dynamics. Such practice must be grounded in careful reflection of the situation. Indeed, teachers need to be offered better tools and lenses for closely observing and analyzing the social contexts of their classrooms.

Socratic Disposition

The Socratic disposition represents a paradox of sorts. As the story is told by Plato, Socrates' friend, Chaerephon, asked the oracle at Delphi if anyone was wiser than Socrates. The oracle indicated there was no one wiser. Upon learning this, Socrates dismissed the claim that he was the wisest, recognizing that he knew nothing and many others must be wiser than he. Socrates then set out to find the wiser politicians, poets, and craftsmen to prove he was indeed not the wisest. But in questioning them he realized that they claimed knowledge they did not possess while he had claimed to have no knowledge. That humble insight, he came to see, was the reason he was declared the wisest. The Socratic disposition, therefore, is a stance of humility that recognizes that there is much to learn; this is the heart of wisdom.

Furthering this paradox is the notion that for teachers to take this humble stance requires both courage and confidence. Cornell West (2004) wrote: "[T]he Socratic love of wisdom holds not only that the unexamined life is not worth living (Apology 38a), but also that to be human . . . requires that one must have the courage to think critically for oneself" (p. 208). It takes courage for teachers to critically examine their own practice and look for inconsistencies and weaknesses. This courage to become vulnerable and humble about their pedagogical practice paradoxically grows out of a deeper sense of confidence. The greater the pedagogical wisdom and efficacy, the greater the teacher's awareness becomes of all that yet has to be learned.

The Socratic disposition is one that adopts a disposition towards mastering the craft of teaching. Daniel Pink described mastery using the metaphor of an asymptote, a geometric curve that approaches a straight line without ever reaching it:

> This is the nature of mastery: *Mastery is an asymptote.* You can approach it. You can home in on it. You can get really, really, close to it. . . . The mastery asymptote is a source of frustration. Why reach for something you can never fully attain? But it's also a source of allure. Why *not* reach for it? The joy is in the pursuit more than the realization. In the end, mastery attracts precisely because mastery eludes. (Pink, 2009, p. 127, emphasis in original)

Mastery as an asymptote is the Socratic disposition. As one becomes more competent and confident in one's abilities, one also recognizes the many areas in which one can improve even further. One increases in confidence and humility simultaneously. This is the paradox of mastery.

We argue that the most effective coaches and teachers maintain this Socratic disposition. They are never content. They know that they can improve and are often the most critical of their own performance. Despite the accomplishments outlined in this volume, the coaches and teachers presented here also make themselves vulnerable by sharing their reflection of their own practice. For example, Coach Cann shared her failure to build a winning club volleyball team around star players. Through a Socratic disposition, she came to see that she could not build a team culture in this way. It was a lesson she took with her when she entered the classroom.

Coach DeMeulenaere attempted to inspire his players to work hard in practice. Despite trying multiple tactics, he remained dissatisfied and continued to look for answers; he realized that the key to success fell on the shoulders of a leader in their midst. Despite some progress, he continued to critically examine his practice like a social scientist, maintaining that relentless drive to continually improve.

Similarly, Coach Malone learned to courageously accept that he wasn't reaching all of his students; the poor writing skills of his students reflected the shortcomings in his teaching despite the teaching award that he had received. He knew that he had to look honestly and courageously at his own practice to find the answers that would help his students improve their writing. This is the essence of praxis.

These coaches practiced the praxis required of effective pedagogues. They carefully read the social dynamics in their classrooms and on their teams in order to understand how to improve. And, despite progress, they maintained the humility of the Socratic disposition, knowing they had much more to learn in their quest for mastery.

Implications

The lessons learned from the field have implications for the policy arena in education. While this book, at its center, focuses on effective coaching, the themes drawn from the narratives complicate simplistic understandings about effective pedagogy in urban schools. Here we explicitly bring these points to the fore.

The first point and an underlying premise of this book is that the educational reform movement has misused the metaphor of coaching in education. Ted Sizer offered a powerful way of using athletic coaching as a means to reconceptualize the work of teaching. Educational policymakers appropriated the terms while ignoring insights the metaphor offers. In this book, we have sought to reclaim this metaphor. We have explored the lessons that athletic coaches bring into their own classrooms to become more effective teachers. Sizer wanted coaching to inform how we teach in schools. We affirm that stance and hope that teachers everywhere will embrace these coaches' "lessons from the field."

Second, these narratives offered a challenge to the assumption in current education reform that more metrics provide the map to the elusive golden egg of higher performance. The question raised in these narratives on the field and in the classroom is whether we, as a community, choose to support teachers' efforts through increased funding or deride their efforts through more "teacher bashing." We argue that teachers know what is lacking in their classrooms and their students' performance through the use of authentic assessments, but they need the support to make necessary changes. More statistical data on urban schools to identify "bad teachers" will not produce the needed change. Publicly advertising student test scores to identify "shortcomings" in student populations, teachers or schools only serves to humiliate communities. Humiliation does not effect change; if that were so, then the 90–6 loss alone would have been enough to inspire growth in Coach Malone's basketball players.

Third, because relationships with students and families matter and such relationships are undermined by the false care offered by schools, teachers may need to become outlaws in their schools. Students clearly see the distinction between the authentic, hard caring of *educación* and the aesthetic caring that is so prevalent in schools. The teachers in this volume recognized that they worked for their students and families, not for the school district. It is about seeing players and students as our own children rather than "other people's children" (Delpit, 2006). Becoming allies of youth requires more courage and risk-taking by authentically caring teachers.

In offering these implications and lessons from the field, we have sought to reclaim the metaphor of the teacher as coach, introduced three decades ago. The authors of this volume are deeply appreciative of the lessons derived from the field and court as coaches. Coaching improved our teaching. We hope, in sharing and analyzing these lessons, that we inspire educators to improve their instruction on the field and in the classroom.

References

Antrop-González, R., & De Jesús, A. (2006). Toward a theory of *critical care* in urban small school reform: Examining structures and pedagogies of caring in two Latino community based schools. *The International Journal of Qualitative Studies in Education, 19*(4), 409–433.

Ayers, B., Kumashiro, K., Meiners E., Quinn, T., & Stovall, D. (2010). *Teaching toward democracy: Activism toolkit series.* Boulder, CO: Paradigm Publishers.

Ayvazian, A. (2007). Ending the cycle of oppression: The role of allies as agents of change. In P. S. Rothenberg (Ed.), *Race, class, and gender in the United States: An integrated study* (pp. 724–729). New York, NY: Worth Publishers.

Bennett, W. J. (1993, March 15). Quantifying America's decline. *Wall Street Journal.* Retrieved from http://www.columbia.edu/cu/augustine/arch/usadecline.html

Berger, J., Cohen, B. P., & Zelditch, M., Jr. (1966). Status characteristics and expectation states. In J. Berger, M. Zelditch, Jr., & B. Anderson (Eds.), *Sociological theories in progress* (pp. 29–46). Boston, MA: Houghton Mifflin.

Berger, J., Cohen, B. P., & Zelditch, M., Jr. (1972). Status characteristics and expectation states. *American Sociological Review, 37,* 241–255.

Bloom, A. (1988). *The closing of the American mind.* New York, NY: Simon & Schuster.

Bolton, G. (2010). *Reflective practice: Writing and professional development* (3rd ed.). Thousand Oaks, CA: Sage Publications.

Bourne, R. (1914, November 7). In a schoolroom. *The New Republic,* 23–24.

Bowles, S., & Gintis, H. (1976). *Schooling in capitalist America: Educational reform and the contradictions of economic life.* New York, NY: Basic Books.

Brill, F. S. (2008). *Leading and learning: Effective school leadership through reflective storytelling and inquiry.* Portland, OR: Stenhouse Publishers.

Reflections From the Field, pages 95–99
Copyright © 2013 by Information Age Publishing

Bruner, J. (1996). *The culture of education.* Cambridge, MA: Harvard University Press.

Bruning, R. H., Schraw, G. J., & Ronning, R. R. (1999). *Cognitive psychology and instruction.* Upper Saddle River, NJ: Merrill.

Burdell, P., & Swadner, B. (1999). Critical personal narrative and autoethnography in education: Reflections on a genre. *Educational Researcher, 28*(6), 21–26.

Bushaw, W. J., & McNee, J. A. (2009). The 41st annual Phi Delta Kappan/Gallup poll of the public's attitudes toward public schools. *Phi Delta Kappan, 91*(1), 8–23.

Cann, C. (2012). In search of equity: Teacher tracking in math. In S. Kelly (Ed.), *Assessing teacher quality: Understanding teacher effects on instruction and achievement* (pp. 111–136). New York, NY: Teachers College Press.

Cazden, C. (2001). *Classroom discourse: The language of teaching and learning.* Portsmouth, NH: Heinemann.

Chase, S. E. (2005). Narrative inquiry: Multiple lenses, approaches, voices. In N. K. Denzin & Y. S. Lincoln (Eds.), *The Sage handbook of qualitative research* (3rd ed., pp. 651–679). Thousand Oaks, CA: Sage Publications Inc.

Christensen, F. (1963). A generative rhetoric of the sentence. *College Composition and Communication, 14*(3), 155–161.

Cohen, E., & Lotan, R. (1995). Producing equal status interaction in the heterogeneous classroom. *American Educational Research Journal, 32*(1), 99–120.

Cohen, E., Lotan, R., & Leechor, C. (1989). Can classrooms learn? *Sociology of Education, 62,* 75–94.

Cohen, E., Lotan, R., Scarloss, B., & Arellano, A. (1999). Complex instruction: Equity in cooperative learning classrooms. *Theory into Practice, 38,* 80–86.

Collins, J. (2001). *Good to great: Why some companies make the leap . . . and others don't.* New York, NY: HarperCollins.

Cone, J. (2006, Winter). Detracked ninth-grade English: Apprenticeship for the work and world of high school and beyond. *Theory into Practice, 45*(1), 55–63.

Delpit, L. (1988). The silenced dialogue: Power and pedagogy in educating other people's children. *Harvard Educational Review, 58*(3), 280–298.

Delpit, L. (2006). *Other people's children: Cultural conflict in the classroom.* New York, NY: New Press.

DeMeulenaere, E. (2012). Toward a pedagogy of trust. In C. Dudley-Martin & S. Michaels (Eds.), *High-expectation curricula: Helping all students succeed with powerful learning* (pp. 28–41). New York, NY: Teachers College Press.

Denzin, N. K., Lincoln, Y., & Rolling Jr., J. H. (2006). Special issue on autoethnography, critical race theory, and performance studies. *Qualitative Inquiry, 12*(2), 427–429.

Dewey, J. (1897). My pedagogic creed. *School Journal, 54,* 77–80.

Dillon, S. (2011, March 6). Tight budgets mean squeeze in classrooms. *New York Times.* Retrieved from New York Times Company: http://www.nytimes.com/2011/03/07/education/07classrooms.html?pagewanted=all

Donovan, M. S., & Bransford, J. D. (2005). Introduction. In M. S. Donovan & J. D. Bransford (Eds.), *How students learn: History, mathematics, and science in the classroom* (pp. 1–30). Washington, DC: The National Academies Press.

Drewe, S. B. (2000). An examination of the relationship between coaching and teaching. *Quest, 52,* 79–88.

Duncan, M. (2004). Autoethnography: Critical appreciation of an emerging art. *International Journal of Qualitative Methods, 3*(4), Article 3. Retrieved from http://www.ualberta.ca/~iiqm/backissues/3_4/pdf/duncan.pdf

Duncan-Andrade, J. M. R. (2010). *What a coach can teach a teacher: Lessons urban schools can learn from a successful sports program.* New York, NY: Peter Lang.

Duncan-Andrade, J. M. R., & Morrell, E. (2008). *The art of critical pedagogy: Possibilities for moving from theory to practice in urban schools.* New York, NY: Peter Lang.

Dweck, C. S. (2006). *Mindset: The new psychology of success.* New York, NY: Random House.

Eggen, P., & Kauchak D. (2001). *Educational psychology: Windows on classrooms.* Upper Saddle River, New Jersey: Prentice Hall.

Ellis, C. (2004). *The ethnographic I: A methodological novel about autoethnography.* Walnut Creek, CA: AltaMira Press.

Ellis, C., & Bochner, A.P. (2000). Autoethnography, personal narrative, reflexivity: Researcher as subject. In N. K. Denzin & Y. S Lincoln (Eds.), *The handbook of qualitative research* (2nd ed., pp. 733–768). Thousand Oaks, CA: Sage.

Fine, M. (1991). *Framing dropouts: Notes on the politics of an urban high school.* Albany, NY: State University of New York Press.

Foucault, M. (1995). *Discipline and punish: The birth of the prison.* (A. Sheridan, Trans.). New York, NY: Random House. (Original work published 1975.)

Freire, P. (1970). *Pedagogy of the oppressed.* New York, NY: Continuum.

Freire, P. (1993). *Pedagogy of the city.* New York, NY: Continuum.

Gallimore, R., & Tharp, R. (2004). What a coach can teach a teacher, 1975–2004: Reflections and reanalysis of John Wooden's teaching practices. *The Sport Psychologist, 18*(2), 119–137.

Giroux, H. (1983). Theories of reproduction and resistance in the new sociology of education: A critical analysis. *Harvard Educational Review, 53*(3), 257–293.

Glenn, J. M. L. (2002). Stepping out of the spotlight: What teachers can learn from coaches. *Business Education Forum, 57*(2), 8–13.

Gruwell, E. (2007). *The gigantic book of teachers' wisdom.* New York, NY: Skyhorse Publishing.

Haberman, M. (1991). The pedagogy of poverty versus good teaching. *Phi Delta Kappan, 73*(4), 290–294.

Haberman, M. (2010). Consequences of failing to address the pedagogy of poverty. *Phi Delta Kappan, 92*(2), 45.

Harris, R. (1989). How does writing restructure thought? *Language and Communication, 9*(2/3), 99–106.

Heath, S. B., & Langman, J. (1994). Shared thinking and the register of coaching. In D. Biber & F. Finegan (Eds.), *Sociolinguistic perspectives on register* (pp. 82–105). New York, NY: Oxford University Press.

Holt, D. (1999). What coaching football taught me about teaching writing. *The Voice, 4*(3), 5, 13.

Horn, I. S. (2006). Lessons learned from detracked mathematics departments. *Theory into Practice, 45*(1), 72–81.

Johnson, J., Carlson, S., Kastl, J., & Kastl, R. (1992). Developing conceptual thinking: The concept attainment model. *The Clearing House, 66*(2), 117–121.

Kaufman, P., & Wolff, E. A. (2010). Playing and protesting: Sport as a vehicle for social change. *Journal of Sport and Social Issues, 34*(2), 154–175.

Kesey, K. (1963). *One flew over the cuckoo's nest.* New York, NY: Signet.

Kohl, H. (1994). *"I won't learn from you" and other thoughts on creative maladjustment.* New York, NY: The New Press.

Kohl, H. (2009). The educational panopticon. *Teachers College Record.* Retrieved from http://tcrecord.org ID number: 15477.

Kohn, A. (2012). Test today, privatize tomorrow: Using accountability to "reform" public schools to death. In W. Watkins (Ed.), *The assault on public education: Confronting the politics of corporate school reform* (pp. 79–96). New York, NY: Teachers College Press.

Ladson-Billings, G. (1994). *The dreamkeepers: Successful teachers for African-American children.* San Francisco, CA: Jossey-Bass.

Ladson-Billings, G. (2006). From the achievement gap to the education debt: Understanding achievement in U.S. schools. *Educational Researcher, 35*(7), 3–12.

Lave, J., & Wenger, E. (1991). *Situated learning: Legitimate peripheral participation.* Cambridge, UK: Cambridge University Press.

Marzano, R. J., Marzano, J. S., & Pickering, D. J. (2003). *Classroom management that works: Research-based strategies for every teacher.* Alexandria, VA: Association for Supervision and Curriculum Development.

Menary, R. (2007). Writing as thinking. *Language Sciences, 29*, 621–632

Murphy, J., & Datnow, A. (2003). *Leadership lessons from comprehensive school reforms.* Thousand Oaks, CA: Corwin Press.

Neufeld, B., & Roper, D. (2003). *Coaching: A strategy for developing instructional capacity, promises, and practicalities.* Washington, DC: Aspen Institute Program on Education and Providence, RI: Annenberg Institute for School Reform.

Noddings, N. (2008). Caring and peace education. In M. Bajaj (Ed.), *The encyclopedia of peace education* (pp. 87–92). Charlotte, NC: Information Age Publishing.

Oakes, J. (1985). *Keeping track: How schools structure inequality.* New Haven, CT: Yale University Press.

Olegario, M. (2007, November 10). The pack is back. Retrieved from http://mikeoleg.blogspot.com/2007/11/pack-is-back.html

Owen, W. (2011, September 5). Crowded Portland-area classrooms force teachers to cope so students can learn. *The Oregonian.* Retrieved from http://www.oregonlive.com/education/index.ssf/2011/09/crowded_portland_area_classroo.html

Pink, D. (2009). *Drive: The surprising truth about what motivates us.* New York, NY: Riverhead Books.

Segal, J. Z. (1996). Pedagogies of decentering and a discourse of failure. *Rhetoric Review, 15*(1), 174–191.

Sizer, T. (1984). *Horace's compromise.* Boston, MA: Houghton-Mifflin.

Stellwagon, J. B. (1997). The teacher as coach: Re-thinking a popular educational paradigm. *The Clearing House, 70,* 271–273.

Valenzuela, A. (1999). *Subtractive schooling: U.S. Mexican youth and the politics of caring.* Albany, NY: State University of New York Press.

Valenzuela, A. (2005). Subtractive schooling, caring relations, and social capital in the schooling of U.S.-Mexican youth. In L. Weis & M. Fine (Eds.), *Beyond silenced voices: Class, race, and gender in United States schools* (pp. 83–94). Albany, NY: State University of New York Press.

Wall, S. (2006). An autoethnography on learning about autoethnography. *International Journal of Qualitative Methods, 5*(2), Article 9. Retrieved from http://www.ualberta.ca/~iiqm/backissues/5_2/html/wall.htm

Watanabe, M., Nunes, N., Mebane, S., Scalise, K., & Claesgens, J. (2007). "Chemistry for all instead of chemistry just for the elite": Lessons learned from detracked chemistry classrooms. *Science Education, 91*(5), 683–709.

Wenger, E. (1998). *Communities of practice: Learning, meaning, and identity.* New York, NY: Cambridge University Press.

Wenger, E. (2003). Communities of practice and social learning systems. In D. Nicolini, S. Gherardi, & D. Yanow (Eds.) *Knowing in organizations: A practice-based approach.* Armonk, NY: M.E. Sharpe.

West, C. (2004). *Democracy matters: Winning the fight against imperialism.* New York, NY: Penguin Press.

Williams, S. (2011, May 8). Seven leadership lessons from Phil Jackson's coaching career. Retrieved from http://www.bigisthenewsmall.com/2011/05/08/7-leadership-lessons-from-phil-jacksons-coaching-career

Willis, P. (1981). *Learning to labor: How working class kids get working class jobs.* New York, NY: Columbia University Press.

Woodson, C. G. (1933). *The mis-education of the Negro.* Washington, DC: Associated Publishers.

Zemelman, S., Daniels, H., & Hyde, A. (2012). *Best practice: Bringing standards to life in America's classrooms* (4th ed.). Portsmouth, NH: Heinemann.

About the Authors

Eric J. DeMeulenaere is an assistant professor of urban schooling in Clark University's education department. Prior to joining Clark University's faculty, he taught middle and high school social studies and English in Oakland and San Francisco, CA, where he also coached soccer. In 2004, he co-founded and directed an innovative small public school in East Oakland that focused on social justice and increased academic outcomes for youth of color. Before opening the school, Dr. DeMeulenaere earned his PhD in the social and cultural studies program at the University of California Berkeley's Graduate School of Education. He has consulted with urban school leaders and teachers nationally and internationally to transform their organizational school cultures. His research employs participatory action research and narrative inquiry methods and draws extensively from critical theory to examine how to create more effective and liberatory learning spaces for urban youth. He lives in Worcester, Massachusetts with his family.

Colette N. Cann is an assistant professor of education and Africana studies at Vassar College where she teaches pre-service teachers and leads initiatives that partner the college with local youth organizations. She taught high school mathematics and coached varsity and junior varsity volleyball after graduating with a B.A. from Stanford University. She received her M.A. in educational policy and PhD in social and cultural studies from the Graduate School of Education at U.C. Berkeley. Dr. Cann completed her post-doctoral research at Stanford University as an Institute of Educational Sciences (U.S. Department of Education) scholar. Her own research examines

Reflections From the Field, pages 101–102
Copyright © 2013 by Information Age Publishing

college–K12 school partnerships and racialized campus events in higher education. Her most recent publications include a collective autoethnography on activism in academia and a mixed methods study on teacher tracking in secondary mathematics departments.

CPSIA information can be obtained at www.ICGtesting.com
Printed in the USA
BVOW001813070413

317517BV00002B/19/P

9 781623 962685